6-99

BFI FILM (
....

Edward B
S E R I E S

Colin MacCabe an ....

S E R I E S C O N S U L T A N T S

D1495031

Cinema is a fragile medium. Many of the great classic films of the past now exist, if at all, in damaged or incomplete prints. Concerned about the deterioration in the physical state of our film heritage, the National Film and Television Archive, a Division of the British Film Institute, has compiled a list of 360 key films in the history of the cinema. The long-term goal of the Archive is to build a collection of perfect show-prints of these films, which will then be screened regularly at the Museum of the Moving Image in London in a year-round repertory.

BFI Film Classics is a series of books commissioned to stand alongside these titles. Authors, including film critics and scholars, film-makers, novelists, historians and those distinguished in the arts, have been invited to write on a film of their choice, drawn from the Archive's list. Each volume presents the author's own insights into the chosen film, together with a brief production history and a detailed filmography, notes and bibliography. The numerous illustrations have been specially made from the Archive's own prints.

With new titles published each year, the BFI Film Classics series will rapidly grow into an authoritative and highly readable guide to the great films of world cinema.

Could scarcely be improved upon ... informative, intelligent, jargon-free companions.
The Observer

Cannily but elegantly packaged BFI Classics will make for a neat addition to the most discerning shelves.
New Statesman & Society

75076

Garbo as Christina

BFI FILM
CLASSICS

QUEEN CHRISTINA

....

Marcia Landy & Amy Villarejo

BRITISH FILM INSTITUTE

bfi

BFI PUBLISHING

First published in 1995 by the
BRITISH FILM INSTITUTE
21 Stephen Street, London W1P 2LN

The British Film Institute exists
to promote appreciation, enjoyment, protection and
development of moving image culture in and throughout
the whole of the United Kingdom.
Its activities include the National Film and
Television Archive; the National Film Theatre;
the Museum of the Moving Image;
the London Film Festival; the production and
distribution of film and video; funding and
support for regional activities;
Library and Information Services;
Stills, Posters and Designs; Research,
Publishing and Education; and the monthly
Sight and Sound magazine.

British Library Cataloguing-in-Publication Data
A catalogue record for this book is available from the British Library

ISBN 0-85170-523-5

Designed by
Andrew Barron & Collis Clements Associates

Typesetting by
Fakenham Photosetting Limited, Norfolk

Printed in Great Britain by
The Trinity Press, Worcester

CONTENTS

ACKNOWLEDGMENTS

We would like to express our gratitude to colleagues and friends who assisted in the research and preparation of the manuscript. Particularly, we are appreciative of Ed Buscombe's careful reading of the work and for his extremely helpful suggestions for its improvement. We are grateful to the staff at the Academy of Motion Picture Arts and Sciences for making a wealth of archival material from and about the film available to us and for permission to reproduce stills from *Queen Christina* and publicity shots from the film. Kathy Lendech of Turner Entertainment Company was most understanding in helping us to acquire further permissions from Turner for use of the stills. The staff at the Museum of Modern Art in New York assisted us in tracking down contemporary reviews of the film.

Our special thanks to Colin MacCabe for his encouragement of the project, his helpful critical insight, and his friendship. We are grateful to Lucy Fischer, Director of the Film Studies Program at the University of Pittsburgh, for fostering a creative environment for cinema studies. We appreciate the support of Mary Louise Briscoe, Dean of the College of Arts and Sciences and Philip Smith, Chairman of the English Department. We would like to thank each other for making collaborative work intellectually exciting, pleasurable, and possible. We would also like to thank Stanley Shostak for his support of intellectual work and for his friendship and we express our special appreciation to Don and Merna Villarejo for their support and Vanessa and Wat for their unflagging companionship.

Rouben Mamoulian (rt) on set with Garbo and Gilbert

'QUEEN CHRISTINA'
. . . .

From her first US silent film, *The Torrent* (1926), Greta Garbo was the property of Metro-Goldwyn-Mayer, the studio that boasted 'more stars than there were in heaven'. Unlike silent stars such as Pola Negri, she not only made the transition to sound in *Anna Christie* (1930) – in both English and German – but went on to achieve even greater acclaim for her roles in sound films. Filmgoers responded to the fit between her screen persona as the tragic lover and her throaty, accented voice pronouncing her famous first line: 'Gimme a whiskey, ginger ale on the side, and don't be stingy, baby.' She was a lucrative asset for the studio, and her relations with mogul Louis B. Mayer and his young assistant Irving Thalberg assured her of a certain type of publicity, one which worked in the direction of protecting her privacy. She was permitted minimum exposure to the press, allowing the studio to handle her image. She was not, however, a docile star, and when her contract ended in 1932, she drove a hard bargain with Mayer, refusing to return to work for eighteen months ('I tink I go home,' she is reported to have said to Mayer as she left for Sweden). The studio ultimately relented and gave her the money she demanded, as well as greater power over her films. Along with the $250,000 she was to receive for each picture, she was permitted veto power over names of directors submitted for her approval as well as screenwriters and actors who were to appear in the films.[1]

In late 1932, when the studio began pre-production for *Queen Christina*, she had what in effect amounted to her own production company.[2] When she learned that the studio gave her a choice between Edmund Goulding and Robert Z. Leonard as director for *Queen Christina*, she chose Goulding, who, as it turned out, was not available. Ernst Lubitsch was then suggested as a possibility, and Garbo expressed her preference for him over Leonard. Other names the studio considered were Jack Conway, Sam Wood and even Josef von Sternberg, who was working with Marlene Dietrich on *The Scarlet Empress* at the time. Finally, when the studio proposed Rouben Mamoulian, Garbo cabled to them, 'Approve Mamoulian', and although his price was initially unacceptable to Mayer, MGM finally enlisted him for *Queen Christina*.

Rouben Mamoulian was, like Garbo, an immigrant to

Hollywood. Born in Russia, he studied criminal law at Moscow University and then worked at the Moscow Art Theatre. He went to the US to direct the American Opera Company in Rochester, New York, and moved west in the late 1920s. His first assignment in Hollywood was *Applause* in 1929, and he established himself as an innovative sound director, 'liberating both camera and sound track'.[3] He recalled that he had been brought to Hollywood 'as a stage expert on dialogue, and all I could think of was the marvellous things one could do with the cameras and the exciting new potentials of sound recording'.[4] Later, he experimented with the dramatic use of colour in *Becky Sharp* (1935). According to Tom Milne, by the time Mamoulian was asked to direct *Queen Christina* he was a 'gilt-edged property snatched from Paramount'.[5] His work on the Garbo film abounds with instances of his innovative handling of the melodrama which, like his experimentation with sound on film, may be accounted for by his operatic background. Garbo's approval of him reflects her ability to select individuals who would enhance her performance. While Mamoulian's desire for complete control over his projects might have conflicted with Garbo's star prerogatives, his preoccupation with women's struggles, evident in his entire *oeuvre*, enhanced his fit with the *Queen Christina* project, and the two ultimately worked extremely well together.[6]

In seeking to elevate Mamoulian to the status of an *auteur*, Mark Spergel, in his biography of Mamoulian, identifies as the director's major preoccupation a dramatic conflict between instinctual drives and a 'nobler potential for the spiritual, Platonic notion of love'.[7] In many of Mamoulian's films, that conflict is anchored in a woman's struggle against the constraints of convention, as it is in *Queen Christina*. Like the director, Christina will assert the liberating power of art, of higher and nobler thought, to counter mundane and base behaviour. Mamoulian's attraction to the biopic may or may not be reducible to his own life or to the traditional explanatory strategies of psychoanalysis (Spergel attributes special significance to Mamoulian's experiences with a talented and frustrated mother), but it is clear that he was attracted to the project and found both a vehicle through which to express his preoccupations and personnel congenial to his methods of directing.

Initially, Garbo approved the studio's nomination of Laurence Olivier for the part of Don Antonio, the Spanish ambassador and her lover in the film, and she also approved supporting actors Reginald Owen, Ian Keith, C. Aubrey Smith and Lewis Stone. Olivier was also acceptable to Mamoulian, who had originally wanted John Barrymore for the role. The young Olivier and Garbo made a test of a love scene, and a change in the casting of Don Antonio followed immediately. Olivier later commented that he was 'nervous and scared of [his] leading lady. I knew that I was lightweight for her and nowhere near her stature.'[8] All accounts of the test confirm that Garbo found the love scene with Olivier unacceptable and that she requested instead John Gilbert, the enormously popular silent star who had played her leading man in three of her silent films. After Garbo rejected Olivier, others, including Leslie Howard, Franchot Tone, Nils Asther and Bruce Cabot, were considered for the role that eventually went to Gilbert, but they declined or were rejected after screen tests.

John ('Jack') Gilbert came to *Queen Christina* with a tumultuous history regarding both Garbo and the studio. As MGM's leading silent actor, Gilbert had starred with Garbo in the film that established them as a pair, both on screen and off, *Flesh and the Devil* (1926). The passion between them in the film ignited audience interest in the couple, and the Hollywood gossip machine and the studio's own publicity staff fuelled the flame with rumours that they were indeed a real-life 'item'. There is no doubt that there is some truth behind the rumours: Gilbert provided Garbo with a home in Hollywood for many years and instructed her in the minutiae of star life, from dealings with the studio and the press to selecting an agent (they shared Harry Edington throughout their careers). Publicity for their second feature together further stoked the fires of rumour, as the studio retitled their adaptation of *Anna Karenina* as *Love* (1927) to produce the tag line, 'Garbo and Gilbert in *Love*!'

Garbo's Hollywood persona, however, was at odds with images of domesticity and coupledom, representing most often the tragic heroine doomed to a life 'alone', and another much publicised incident added to her reputation as a loner: Garbo stood Gilbert up at the altar in what was meant to be a double wedding between Garbo and Gilbert and King Vidor and Eleanor Boardman. Whatever the substance of their relations, and there is an evidential push-me-pull-you match still raging in biographical accounts, Garbo and Gilbert were a lucrative and highly commodified product of MGM, and the studio exploited their popularity as far as possible. The same studio, however, wielded its power over Jack Gilbert to more sinister ends. In a vendetta admirably documented by Gilbert's daughter, Leatrice Joy Fountain, Louis B. Mayer successfully fought Gilbert's demands for adequate compensation and control over his films through a smear campaign which prohibited Gilbert from moving into sound film almost altogether.[9] *Queen Christina* presented Gilbert with an opportunity to redeem his failing career, and many claim that Garbo's selection of Gilbert was a gracious gesture to a past friend in need. It was rumoured in the press, however, that Garbo had stipulated that there was to be no ardent embrace with Gilbert, and an examination of the film reveals this to be the case. While Gilbert's role in *Queen Christina* failed to boost his career, it provided Garbo with a sympathetic leading man who was a known quantity, able to put her at ease during production.

Another known quantity on the set of *Queen Christina* was William Daniels, Garbo's cameraman for most of her films. Daniels contributed to the identifiable style of MGM films of the early 1930s. This carefully fabricated and glossy style is evident in the studio's creation of star types, especially of its female stars. The scripts and the sleek look of the films were attributable in large part to the quality and consistency of the personnel at the studio: producers, writers and technicians.[10] In retrospect, Daniels found Garbo to be 'definitely the most beautiful woman I ever photographed. Her outstanding characteristic is her eyes. That's why we made so many big close ups – to see what she was thinking.'[11] During his tenure at MGM, Daniels effectively shaped the Garbo look, experimenting with the available technology, especially as regards lighting, to enhance the image of Garbo which was MGM's hottest commodity.

Daniels claimed to have learned a great deal about innovative lighting from Erich von Stroheim, for whom he worked prior to the Garbo films. In his recollections, Daniels describes how he began to experiment with lighting effects on Stroheim films, learning especially to balance light and dark and to play with reflections. Daniels also takes credit for insisting on filming Garbo on closed sets, although the requirement also squares with Garbo's persona of the maniacally private woman. Working on that intensely close terrain, however it came about, allowed Daniels a significant hand in creating the look associated with Garbo's films. He recalls his role, although he may minimise his contribution: 'I didn't create a "Garbo face". I just did portraits of her I would have done for any star. My lighting of her was determined by the requirements of a scene. I didn't, as some say I did, keep one side of the face light and the other dark. But I did always try to make the camera peer into the eyes, to see what was there. Garbo had natural long lashes and in certain moods I could throw the light down from quite high, and show the shadows of the eyelashes come down on her cheeks; it became a sort of trademark with her.'[12]

Daniels further describes the technique he developed for lighting Garbo in the famous bedroom scene in *Queen Christina*: 'All the light came from the fire – or seemed to; of course we had to cheat a little by using special small spotlights that illuminated the bedposts in such a way that they seemed to be like the kind of light the flickering flames would make.'[13] From his work on *Queen Christina* as well as from the bulk of his films with Garbo, it is evident that Daniels studied his subject matter carefully and was eager to do justice to the star as well as to the more general ambience of the film. Clarence Sinclair Bull, Garbo's chief still photographer at MGM, confirms Daniels' assessment of Garbo's photogenic nature: 'She was the most beautiful woman from a camera standpoint I ever photographed. You could shoot her from any angle.'[14]

Adrian, Garbo's dress designer, was another major factor in the creation of what came to be known in the 1930s as the MGM style. His ability to tailor costumes for Garbo's physique and style set fashion rather than followed current trends. 'Garbo isn't very fond of the fashionable hat of the moment, nor is she fond of fashionable hairdos,' he commented in an interview for *Photoplay* magazine.[15] Instead, the costumes he created for Garbo became in his words 'fashion Fords'.[16] As others on the MGM team scrutinised Garbo to enhance her image, Adrian 'studied Garbo like a surgeon would an X-ray. She was big-boned, square-shouldered, mannish. He accentuated these obstacles to femininity and had a great deal to do with her screen success.'[17] As Jane Gaines has discussed at length, Adrian's costumes provided a clue to the film's ambivalent style by offering what she dubs 'a sartorial essay on sexuality and power'.[18] Gaines' reading of the spectacular dimensions of Adrian's costumes suggests how the film diverges from the usual generic requirements of the royal biopic by emphasising the constructed nature of symbolic power, its making and its unmaking.

Gaines' comments on the relation between costume and cultural knowledge, which we will explore at some length in our reading of the film, are also abundantly illustrated in every aspect of the film's production – original sources, initial scripting, readers' reports, costuming, advertising, and even censorship documents.

. . . .

The recollections of the various workers at MGM who were associated with Garbo's films attest to the regard in which Garbo was held and the extreme care with which she was handled. In fact, even the individuals who worked on her scripts were considered 'Garbo specialists', especially Salka Viertel and S. N. Behrman, who were to work on the screenplay and script for *Queen Christina*. According to Viertel, an expatriate from Nazi Germany, a friend as well as a professional colleague of the star, it was Garbo who 'urged me to write the film about Christina' (although, as is characteristic of Hollywood reminiscence, others have also claimed to be the originators of the vehicle for Garbo). Viertel further suggests that it was Garbo who

1 4   Adrian's 'fashion Fords'

brought MGM producer Irving Thalberg to see her, having given him a copy of Viertel's manuscript. 'While he disclaimed interest in historical subjects [an ironic comment for the studio],' Viertel wrote, 'he expressed interest in making the film.'[19]

An analysis of the various versions of the script and screenplay reveals the way in which the material was moulded to suit the screen, the times, and the figure of Garbo herself. The first reader's report on *Queen Christina*, meant to assess the viability of literary material for screen adaptation, is based on Strindberg's *Kønigen Christina*, and Mr Feyder found the subject suitable 'for a temperamental film star'. Strindberg's view of the queen is negative: Christina brings the country to the verge of disaster. Feyder concludes that 'the palace is a brothel' and the queen, 'although brilliant in intellect and dominating in character, has the temperamental and over-sexed character of a great artist'. Ultimately, Feyder dismisses the source, suggesting that 'the play is entirely too involved and has never had more than a literary success'.[20]

Jessie Burns, another reader from the script department, assessed

Faith Compton Mackenzie's *The Sibyl of the North*, finding it suitable 'for a mature actress'. Burns' analysis stresses scenes involving Christina's conflicting relationship with her mother, her preference for southern climes (which engenders Magnus' hatred), her lack of patience with women, her hatred of her role as monarch, her possession of 'a strong masculine quality in her makeup [which] turned her in loathing from marriage' and her unconventional life in Europe after her abdication. Burns concludes that the 'strong and splendid character of Christina is traceable through this version of her life and this itself is colorful picture material. But the compilation of events as here recorded is sketched too broadly to be useful to us except as research. Intimate and personally dramatic accounts would be more useful to us.'[21] As these 'personally dramatic accounts' take shape, they centre on the 'masculine' character of Christina which informs the melodramatic conflict regarding her gender.

Salka Viertel and Margaret 'Peg' LeVino adapted *The Sibyl of the North*, and Burns reports that the adapters 'have done a good job. Even in the inference of Christina's passion for a woman, the scenes are delicately handled so that only the "wise" can get the idea.' She adds too that the 'love that inspired [Christina] finally to abdicate should be a tremendous thing and should possess elements that we feel new to her life.'[22] This initial lengthy treatment by Viertel and LeVino begins with Christina's last years in Rome in 1688, flashes back to her youth in 1626, and inserts her birth and the resulting confusion about her gender.

The script stresses more conflicts around the question of her gender than does the final text, including the young Christina's antipathy to wearing dresses, her conflicts with the regent Axel Oxenstierna, and her great disappointment about Ebba Sparre's love for Count Jacob de la Gardie. This version provides for a great ball where Christina favours Don Antonio, the Spanish ambassador, over Swedish courtiers. The court intrigue and pressure on her to marry against her own desires, the fears over her amorous relationship with Don Antonio, and the court unrest that escalates as a consequence originate in this treatment, as does the abdication.[23] The treatment ends with Don Antonio's and Christina's deaths in Rome, although Bess Meredyth proposed a happy ending with the two lovers united after Christina's abdication.[24]

Viertel and LeVino's initial adaptation did not contain the famous inn scene we find in the final version. The first mention of a scene at the inn with Christina disguised not as a man but as a lower-class woman occurs in the January 1933 script with dialogue. H. M. Harwood joined the team, and his contributions in April of the same year are closer to the final version of the film, although Christina's discovery of the death of Don Antonio still does not take place aboard ship. Both the tightening of the action and the sharpening of the dialogue assume a version closer to the actual film, with Viertel and

Harwood's version of May 1933 and, in the same month, S. N. Behrman's contributions to the dialogue adding witty interchanges and erudite allusions (to Molière, Calderón and Velazquez). The final shooting script is dated 31 July 1933, with changes included from 3 August.

When Garbo returned from her eighteen-month stay in Sweden, she carried with her a suitcase full of reference materials on Queen Christina which she had collected there.[25] But the studio also hired a historical adviser, Colonel Einhornung, whose job was to ensure that Swedish royalty would not take offence to the film. According to Alexander Walker, 'the colonel did so, and his advice was cheerfully ignored by Mamoulian and company'.[26] The colonel had many complaints about the film's historical inaccuracies, among which were the way the queen is quick to go to bed with a stranger and the fact that the Diet ought not to be seen to clamour for war, as is the case in the early scene of Christina and her fire-eating courtiers. In terms of details relating to costuming and to properties, he asserted that nobles did not wear light-coloured hose and short wigs, nor would it have been possible for there to have been (in Sweden's cold climate) the abundant fruits that are displayed in the inn scene. More recently, George Fraser Macdonald has faulted the script for showing an old Gustavus Adolphus dying on the battlefield of Lutzen, since the king was only thirty-eight when he died, and he also points out that the queen's abdication was not the consequence of a romantic entanglement.

These complaints are interesting not only for the light they shed on the ways that biopics – with their predominant concern for spectacle – evolve, but more particularly for the way they echo the familiar grievances of critics about the genre's 'unreliable' treatments of history. The assumption that the objective of the films is to produce an accurate picture of the individuals and the period in question obstructs an analysis of what kind of history it is that the films portray. Critical cavils regarding the biopic are consonant with the view that Hollywood produced frivolous films that falsify 'reality', wreaking havoc with history in favour of 'escapist' entertainment. Notwithstanding this prejudice, which seems to belong to the long-standing refusal to take Hollywood films and their audiences seriously, *Queen Christina* does in fact conform to certain aspects of the history of that period, though selectively, as represented by the queen's 'relentless quest for peace, her distaste for a dynastic marriage, her devotion to scholarship'.[27]

If one regards these historical films from the vantage point of fusing contemporary expectations with versions of the past, it is possible to see that popular history is still history, but a history that is patterned on gossip, folklore and melodrama. The history that is constructed is revealing for the insights it offers into the period in which it is constructed. As the readers' reports on the *Queen Christina* scripts disclose, there is a predilection for popular psychology which shapes the narrative of the 'intimate and personally dramatic' character of Christina not simply according to standards of historical fidelity, but adhering to dominant conceptions of the exceptional individual. To this end, the film bows to the need to assign specific motives to the actions of exceptional individuals, to trace these motives to their childhood experiences, and to locate them in familial relations. The familial is then transposed onto sexual and romantic registers. The biopic is a particularly effective genre through which to orchestrate psychological, familial, religious and political attitudes. In this respect, the evolution of *Queen Christina* follows this trajectory neatly; where it diverges is in its undermining of nationalistic and patriotic models, as we shall discuss in our analysis of the film.

If the conception of history that evolved for the final shooting script is a collage of recorded events from Queen Christina's biography with contemporary embellishments, it is in part due to the necessity of making historical subjects appear 'modern' for film spectators. As for Hollywood history, the biopic seems a form particularly suited to the style of life cultivated in the film world through movie magazines, radio, newspapers, advertisements, the world of fashion, and the Movietone news. An examination of the publicity shots for the film reveals an emphasis on elements of action and adventure, involving Magnus de la Gardie (Ian Keith) and Don Antonio's quarrel and shots of their duel, Garbo in close-up on the throne in the night scene before her abdication, and Garbo and Keith on the ship at the end of the film as she sends him away before she sails.

The MGM Exhibitor's Campaign Book, constructed to provide exhibitors with a variety of information that would be useful in publicising the film in their areas, corroborates the selective uses of history in the film.[28] Along with a list of the players, the book provided brief biographies which stress their theatrical and film experience. The notes confirm Garbo's benevolence towards Gilbert, who is said to have 'retired from the screen to direct and write but was invited by Garbo to return for a role in *Queen Christina*'. The book also makes apparent the foreign origins of a good part of the cast: Garbo, Reginald Owen, David Torrence and Gustav von Seyffertitz.

The Exhibitor's book also provides the distributors and exhibitors with 'catchliners' designed to whet the potential spectator's curiosity. Emphasising the modern dimensions of the historical biopic is the most famous line: 'A Queen whose romance was as modern as tomorrow's tabloids', and, in the same vein, 'A seventeenth century maiden who loved with a twentieth century madness'. Others emphasised the gender confusion which the final shooting script foregrounded: 'She was crowned King of Sweden ... lived and ruled as a man ... But surrendered to Love', and 'They crowned her King of Sweden ... But within her frigid heart a tempestuous lover found an amorous glamorous woman.' As much as the catchliners stressed modern melodramatic concerns, the book supplemented the demand for history (which the studio had itself created) with titbits regarding the film's historical accuracy and authenticity. One blurb boasted that 'historical archives serve as guides for authentic sets in *Queen Christina*' and noted that the details of the old palace that had been 'consumed by flame' were reproduced from descriptions in travel diaries of the period. The book indulged in further advertisement for the film's historical fidelity, waxing enthusiastic on the powers of the studio to 'create' authenticity by noting that the 'stones' of the palace walls were 'aged' by a special process of muddying and that all of the woodwork had received a blush of paint. This publicity thus captures the conjunction of the factual and the spectacular characteristic of the biopic.

The articles in the book emphasise the authentic and spectacular nature of the costumes as well, stressing that it was through paintings of the Christina period that 'authentic information concerning settings and costumes was obtained'. The gown in which Christina formally welcomes Don Antonio to the court is described as 'ivory velvet adorned with bands of silver thread and bits of cut steel and square diamonds'. Don Antonio's costumes were 'based on Velazquez paintings that hang in the Prado'. At the same time that these articles boast historical accuracy, a purported interview with Mamoulian says

Publicity for *Queen Christina*

that 'it is in this respect ... that simplification was most important'. He claims that he did not want the costumes to distract the audience from the performance of the actors. Encapsulating the tension between the historical and the modern, he claims that 'so far as I know, this is the first screen effort toward a modernised treatment of a period story'.

The Exhibitor's book did not limit itself to elements of the film proper; rather it provided support for an advertising onslaught of Christina-related gimmicks. The packet contained a prose serialisation of the film in 'eleven romance-packed chapters' which was scheduled to appear in more than 200 papers. These chapters were available with illustrations from the film to enhance audience interest in the spectacular Garbo. To heighten the intensity of attention to Garbo, the packet also contained reviews from the first screening of the film in New York at the Astor theatre. In particular, the *New York Journal* emphasises the star's fusion with the historical figure: 'Queen Christina is entirely Garbo, and Garbo is entirely Queen Christina.' A review from the *New York Telegraph* completely disregards the other actors, proclaiming that 'the picture is all Garbo'. The efforts of the Exhibitor's book were supplemented by additional publicity: a 'talking billboard' was set up in a prominent lot in Hollywood. Beside the billboard, displaying signatures of celebrities (such as Norma Shearer, Claudette Colbert and Jean Harlow) and with a loudspeaker attached, was a platform where a man periodically broadcast information about the film. In addition, a shop window display featured a replica of the Swedish throne, surrounded by mannequins in women's fashions derived from the film, and an insignia of the royal house of Sweden. Another shop window contained a display of linen surrounding a photograph of Garbo as Christina.

The studio also announced a 'Queen Christina Overture' which would accompany the screening of the film at Grauman's Chinese Theatre, and it tantalised the potential Los Angeles audience for the screening with the suggestion that Garbo herself might appear (although of course she did not). Despite the studio's massive publicity and fanfare, the film's initial reviews recorded some hesitations about its content; one reviewer described the film as 'not suitable for children and adolescents and not a good show for Sundays in small towns. It is mainly an adult picture.'[29] Prior to its release at Christmas 1933, the film had encountered obstacles from the censors, particularly for its treatment of 'adult' matters of sexuality.

....

The film ran into trouble with the censors as early as August 1933. There were a number of objections to the script communicated to the studio, some religious and others pertaining to concerns over sexual innuendo. The reference to Catholics as 'those heretics' was deemed objectionable, as was Christina's line, 'I shall die a bachelor'. Censors demanded that the studio correct 'the tinge of lesbianism in the relationship between Christina and Ebba' by downplaying Christina's displeasure about Ebba's impending marriage and instead foregrounding her disappointment that Ebba will be taken away from Stockholm. The censor did not rest easily, however. 'Even with these changes,' he wrote, 'we assume that you will be careful to avoid anything in the portrayal of this scene which may be construed as lesbianism.'[30] Especially for spectators over the years who have enjoyed the lesbian 'tinge' in *Queen Christina*, it may not come as a surprise that Hollywood censors objected to lesbian representations, but it is striking that this was not their major complaint about the film.

Most of the requests by the censors centre on the bedroom scene at the inn. The idea of an unmarried man and woman alone in the bedroom was certainly considered risqué by the censors and by the moral constituencies to whom they considered themselves accountable. As if a compromising bedroom scene was not enough in itself to raise objection, the double entendres between the players in the inn sequence – Christina, Don Antonio, his manservant, and the chambermaid – address a wide range of sexual and gender positions outside permissible (and chaste) heterosexual limits. The dialogue swerves and toys with characters' and spectators' awareness in allusions to lesbianism, homosexuality, homosocial bonding, and heterosexuality, confounding these limits.

The repartee begins with Elsa the chambermaid's offer of her services to the young man ('Count Dohna', whom the audience knows to be Christina in disguise); 'The master says you're to have everything you need.' Christina's ambiguous response, 'Hmm ... ', at once denies the offer but invites its reiteration, sustaining the game. As Elsa leaves with a wink, she throws the punchline: 'If you should need anything, my room is at the end of the hall.' Moving from this version of lesbian topography, the dialogue switches perspective to Don Antonio's puzzlement over the identity of 'Count Dohna' as he queries, 'Which side do you sleep on, your right or your left?' The AC/DC Count/Christina responds, 'I never thought of it', an answer which proves unsatisfactory to Don Antonio, who persists: 'They say that a man should always sleep on his side to keep his sword arm free. It's hereditary. It's instinct. [Pause]. Aren't you going to undress?' The reverberations of homosocial tension and homosexual desire linger even when Garbo removes her outer shirt and reveals the curve of her breasts, and the evening sequence closes with a fade, leaving the audience in the dark as to what actually transpires in the bed.

The game of sexual/gender identity and disclosure resumes the following morning with the subsequent shot of the bed concealed by the curtains. Antonio's servant Pedro (Akim Tamiroff) enters the room, assuming that his master is still in bed with the Count: 'At what hour will your Lordship get up?' Antonio resolutely and triumphantly responds: 'I shall *not* get up.' After a double take, the servant acquiesces, 'Very good, milord, will you take chocolate?' Don Antonio responds affirmatively, and Pedro asks, 'Will the *other* gentleman take chocolate?' 'Yes,' retorts Don Antonio, and Pedro delivers his punch:

Garbo and Gilbert in the famous bedroom scene

'Very good, milord, two chocolates.' The banter serves to call further attention to the bed, to what is hidden and remains concealed in the sequence, but it also names obliquely a variety of sexual and gender positions and refuses to curb playfulness by solidifying heterosexual union.

After some quibbling about specific language (for instance, the allusion to 'lovers' as opposed to 'sweethearts' in the quarrel of the soldiers over the number of affairs had by the queen, and references to Antonio's 'sleeping manners'), Will H. Hays wrote to Nicholas Schenck on 5 January 1934, asking that '*Queen Christina* be submitted finally for approval in Hollywood'. A letter from Joseph I. Breen to Louis B. Mayer followed three days later, in which Breen took exception to the bedroom scene in the inn. He wrote, 'It is our judgment that the picture is *in violation of the Production Code*', and he listed a number of deletions that he felt necessary. These involve dialogue and action in the bedroom between the maid, Gilbert and Garbo, as well as between Gilbert and Garbo. In particular, he wanted to 'keep Garbo *away entirely from the bed*' and objected to her lying on the bed and 'fondling the pillow'. Breen considered any undressing objectionable, and proffered a religious opposition to the line 'This is how the Lord must have felt when he beheld the finished world with all his creatures ...' These problems were subsequently adjudicated by a jury composed of Ben Kahane, Jesse Lasky and Junior Laemmle, which decided that the film was 'acceptable' in its present form. They wrote that there were changes they might have liked to see but that they 'were satisfied to let the matter lie'. The version screened for the public, then, contained the famous lengthy inn scene, wherein Garbo caresses the many objects in the room, and that version is the one widely circulated today.

From the correspondence it is clear that the censors not only took their jobs as watchdogs seriously, but were not naive about the sexual innuendoes. The film belongs in that twilight zone between the era before the Production Code and the tightening of censorship that was to become more stringent in ensuing years; the comments of the censors, however, as well as the various readings of the shooting script, reveal a sophisticated and complex contestation over sexual representation and more particularly over the image of Garbo. What the letters of the censors confirm is that censorship is not simply a top-down exercise of power from the censors to the studio, but is instead a continual negotiation of the effects of representations of power and sexuality.

In recent years, critics have tackled the questions of sexual representation in *Queen Christina*. Several have focused attention, much as the censors did, on the tantalising issue of the queen's sexuality, but they are keen to find a match between 'Garbo's own bisexual nature'[31] and the queen's lesbian persona. Reading the film as a coded revelation of Garbo's off-screen sexuality, however, attributes too much power to the star herself and slights the ensemble effects that are central to Hollywood and particularly MGM production of the time. The film's flirtations with sexuality, power and transgressive behaviour are integral to many films of the 1930s which are carry-overs from the silent era, and also extend Garbo's screen image from the 1920s, which included elements of foreignness and androgynous conceptions of beauty circulated through Hollywood cinema and its intertexts (magazines, advertising, gossip, rumour). The Hollywood machine was also aware of the need to appeal to different sexual and gendered constituencies, despite the censors' protests. The question, then, is not whether Garbo actually was or was not a lesbian (although that question preoccupies her biographers to this day) but rather how her star image managed to convey the intricacies, complexities and constructed nature of gender and sexuality. Her powerful screen image, which continues to intrigue critics and fans, is not due to the essentialist, absolute, immutable nature of sexuality but rather to the way in which the institution of stardom comes to represent the fluid nature of identity formation.

....

Queen Christina is an important film for understanding the creation of the star image, its power and its resonances for the culture in which it is shaped and circulated. Certainly, it is important to address the role of Garbo, for, as other critics of the time as well as modern critics are quick to recognise, the success of the film and the critical problems posed by it are inextricable from her star image. In many ways, Garbo's visual image and her acting in *Queen Christina* are consonant with her preceding roles. To borrow a composite set of terms attributed to her performance by various critics, Garbo as Christina is 'aloof', 'mysterious', 'glamorous', 'enchanting', 'magic', 'sphinx-like' and 'sensitive'. These terms have also been used to describe her off-screen persona, to support the conflation between her screen persona and her elusive private life. Garbo was the consummate queen of melodrama, and, more than that, in the hands of her directors and of the publicity machines that continued to dog her until her death, she was also an incarnation of the diva/star, itself a phenomenon of the silent era.

As a diva, her on-screen and off-screen performances were operatic. The excess associated with her performances was not of the overstated histrionic type but powerful in its understatement; it resided in often unspoken but highly visible gestures bespeaking desire and longing. Like the diva of the opera, Garbo's persona, because of this understated and undifferentiated sense of personality, time and place, could appeal to widely divergent audiences and transform the often banal specifics of melodrama into performances that resembled music. The province of the diva is the unending saga of loneliness, pain, suffering, misunderstanding and death, the consummate index of melodrama. The form favours unhappy endings, regarded as exquisite, mysterious and beautiful, over happy ones. In the case of *Queen Christina*, while Garbo's role exposes the unsatisfactory and uncomfortable nature of sexuality within the constraints of social life, revealing contradictions between desire and its realisation, the film does not offer an alternative that is 'happy'. Christina's woeful passage from Sweden to the uncharted seas of Europe entails a journey of loss, death and, above all, uncertainty. This is the terrain of the diva.

In most of her films, Garbo was licensed to suffer, to remain alone and discontented, since simple romance endings were inadequate to the excessiveness of her persona. In *Queen Christina*, the drama hinges inexorably on the diva's inability to reconcile personal life with the rigorous and delimiting demands of the queen's role under the hostile pressures of her courtiers. The demands of serving the nation are conjoined to the question of succession: the queen's duty to marry, and to do so appropriately to preserve the lines of racial purity by marrying a Swedish aristocrat rather than a foreigner. But these injunctions are all transgressed by Christina's refusal to marry ('I shall die a bachelor'), her relationship with the Spaniard, Don Antonio, and her abdication of the throne to her cousin, Charles Augustus, leaving her bereft of kingdom, conjugal relations and maternity.

The points of affinity between the Garbo persona and that of Queen Christina are multiplied in the film. As is characteristic of the diva, Garbo is associated with an adamant refusal to assimilate into the commonplace, to live up to the expectations of others. The parallel between Garbo's legendary refusal to blend into the Hollywood scene and the queen's refusal to abide by the rules prescribed by her royal role was embedded early in the construction of the film. In fact, in early versions of the scenario, one treatment shows Christina's deliberate refusal to attend a ball over which she is to preside, mimicking the dialectic between hiding and disclosure which structured her image throughout her life. In the final version of the script, and in the film as we see it today, the tension between the queen as public persona and Christina as 'private woman' provides the central structuring binary, articulated through every element of the film's form, from costuming to cinematography to *mise en scène*.

The most legendary aspect of Garbo concerns her beauty and especially the exceptional nature of her face. Although she withheld her presence from reviewers and fans, her face was abundantly photographed by studio photographers and these images were circulated to the press. While the close-up is a major factor in star personification, Garbo's face particularly became a subject of fascination, indeed obsession, for her critics, eager to decipher it for clues to her elusive image. Garbo's face is certainly one element of the orchestrated image of Garbo in *Queen Christina*, but the film also makes visible the stance of her body and the slight gestures that are expressive of her state of mind. The film's rhythmic editing measures and stylises Garbo's postures and movements. Acknowledging his use of music on the set, Mamoulian confessed that he used all manner of sound in anti-naturalistic fashion to 'achieve effects that would be impossible and unnatural in real life, yet meaningful and eloquent on the screen'.[32] He also shot some scenes in *Queen Christina* to a metronome to achieve a rhythmic quality akin to a dance.[33]

One of the major characteristics of melodrama, as Peter Brooks and Christine Gledhill have both emphasised, is its mute quality: the fact that verbal language is inadequate to the affect that melodrama seeks to communicate. Hence film melodrama shares a kinship with the operatic, involving not only *melos*, the music, but also gesture, dance and physical nuance, which carry the excess and the contradictions surrounding the characters' struggles with a world which is unyielding. 'Words, however unrepressed and pure, however transparent as vehicles for the expression of basic relations and verities,' writes Peter Brooks, 'appear to be not wholly adequate to the representation of meanings, and the melodramatic message must be formulated through other registers of the sign.'[34] Gesture, posture and facial expressions are indicative of the limits of existing discourse, pointing the way to other modes of experience that cannot be articulated within the constraints of verbal language.

Garbo's acting confirms the idea of melodrama as a transformation of the commonplace into the exceptional. Garbo's pre-eminence as the queen of melodrama derives from the language not only of silent cinema and pantomime but also from opera as a discourse that exceeds the familiar and everyday and registers a heightened affective charge. More than with other stars, critics have focused on Garbo's voice: its timbre, its husky quality and its accent, which signified the foreign and the exotic. That sound, along with her facial expressions and gestures, overrides the constraints of the narrative; her speeches are more like arias than everyday language. This combined effect has led to a consensus that Garbo was exceptional in films that were mediocre vehicles, that she attained a quality of remoteness that exceeds the actual quality of the films. Melodramatic narratives hinge on their obviousness, if not their banality within a familiar range of conflicts, and what distinguishes them is the sense of straining to express the inexpressible, which can only emerge from the nature of the actors' performances and their orchestration.

The quality of remoteness and inaccessibility attributed to Garbo is therefore not mystical, but has a great deal to do with her foreignness. Like the Sternberg films of Marlene Dietrich (brought to Hollywood from Germany and publicised as a competitor to Garbo), Garbo's films belong to a certain moment in Hollywood which was still identified with the old world. The ties to Europe, a Europe associated with culture, wealth and aristocracy, were still intact when Garbo made *Queen Christina*; but, as Christian Viviani points out in an analysis of Hollywood maternal melodramas in the 1930s, important changes were taking place in relation to representations of Europe and especially in relation to questions of sexual morality that were ultimately to affect the careers of Garbo and Dietrich. In particular, these changes involved a greater investment in the Americanisation of stars and in the selection and treatment of film narratives.[35]

That *Queen Christina* did not fare as well at the US box office as was hoped (though it did better in Europe) may be because of this transitional moment in Hollywood's ties to Europe as well as to a number of other factors related to political and social changes. For example, as a consequence of the Depression, immigration came to be regarded as a threat to a shrinking work force in America, and 'foreignness' therefore ceased to signify desirable metropolitan European sophistication. An emphasis on nationalism – 'America first' – may also be understood as a response to the threat of fascism and possibly to impending war in Europe. This nationalism would obviously intensify during the war years. Hollywood films, moreover, also shifted focus from an emphasis on maturity to an inflection on youthfulness, as exemplified in the films of Shirley Temple, Deanna Durbin and, later, Judy Garland. American settings and American motifs, the simple virtues of Main Street Americana, were increasingly the order of the day. Garbo's films, if not specifically identified with Europe, were more generally associated with a European ethos, a sophistication and world-weary maturity that sat in striking contrast to the wide-eyed innocence and seeming immediacy of these younger stars. When the studio demanded that Garbo was to emulate this good-natured and buoyant American charm for her last film, *Two-Faced Woman* (1941), the box-office results were disastrous. Unfortunately, the film's reputation as a disaster still lingers, foreclosing considerations of its merits. *Queen Christina* was, however, potentially still close enough to the immigrant experience and within the orbit of many of the woman's films of the 1930s to resonate with audiences. Garbo's accent, while marked and distinctly identified as Swedish, seemed to signify inaccessibility more than a specific and concrete notion of foreignness. It offered, to many, a representation of a merging of national differences.

Mamoulian's reference to the film as 'a modernised treatment of a period story' seems designed also to counteract any sense in which the film is too narrowly geared to a remote past that has no reference to the audience's experience. The reign of Queen Christina is not presented in terms of issues that are too closely tied to the specific history of Sweden (much to Colonel Einhornung's disappointment) but as transposable to the conflicts of the 1930s. The trajectory of the biopic is geared to melodramatic conflicts that are more generally translatable: a woman's conflict between personal gratification and the demands of society, social obstacles to individual expression, and struggles between romance and service. The thin veneer that separates the conflicts of royalty and the struggles of the stars is evident also in relation to Hollywood history. Fan magazines charted increasing battles between the studio magnates and the stars, and Garbo's struggle for a higher salary and greater control over her films parallels the combative portrait of the queen in the film. A final aspect of the film's 'modernity' resides in its treatment of Sweden's protracted war and particularly the queen's concern over the lavish expenditures demanded by her nobles to maintain the country's greatness, a conflict that spoke to American concerns about nationalism, the need for economy, and the role of the people in guiding national policy in 1933 in the emergent New Deal climate.

The film thus attempts to confront a number of social and cultural issues. The year 1933 and the release of *Queen Christina* seems, however, to mark a turning point for Garbo if measured only in relation to her film of the previous year, *Grand Hotel* (1932–33). That film took forty-nine days to shoot, cost $700,000 and made $947,000, while *Queen Christina* took sixty-eight days to shoot, cost $1,144,000 and made only $632,000.[36] While reviewers heralded *Queen Christina* as a critical success and a success for Garbo, Garbo slipped in the popularity polls from fourth in 1933 (prior to the film's release) to thirty-fourth in the following year. She was not alone in this dramatic change; Dietrich, too, another icon of foreignness, had fallen in popularity.

If 1933 represented a cleft in Garbo's history, the year would also seem to mark a divide in Hollywood history more generally, when the effects of the Depression were making themselves felt in the industry. Reorganisation and retrenchment in the studios had become the order of the day. The decline of audiences, and particularly ethnic audiences in part excluded by the coming of sound, challenged Hollywood film-makers to find ways of resuscitating flagging profits. On the larger political front, fears about the direction of the New Deal in Washington, growing isolationism and especially growing xenophobia were to confront film-makers with new challenges.

The era of expansionism and unlimited prosperity for Hollywood was over. Economic restriction, coupled with greater demands for moral cleansing through the Production Code, made for a tense atmosphere in the movie capital. Attitudes towards the stars within the studios, especially at MGM, were to become more disciplinary, and even the attitudes of the fans seemed to place new demands on the film idols; in relation to Garbo, a *Photoplay* interviewer in 1935 threw to Adrian the much asked question, 'Does Garbo realise that a movie star is public property?'[37] Clearly she did not, and she would resist this demand throughout her life as Christina resists similar attempts on the part of her courtiers and subjects to control her.

The text of *Queen Christina*, then, is a highway for a number of historical events that overarch the specific figure of Greta Garbo and the specific historical events dramatised in the film. The film carries the freight of contemporary conflicts both internal and external to Hollywood. The producers' battles with the Hays Office offer a glimpse of a struggle for a more 'American' morality, expunged of European decadence and fuelled by fan attacks on less conventionally directed ideas of sexual behaviour, specifically relating to romance and marriage in Hollywood representation. In the case of John Gilbert, there is evidence for the disappearance of a certain idea of masculinity which is associated not only with the silent cinema but with more 'gentle' notions of masculinity previously circulated in Hollywood (the new 'king' of MGM would be Clark Gable). In the case of Garbo, one can see in retrospect factors which would ultimately contribute to Garbo's retreat from Hollywood after *Two-Faced Woman* in 1941. And in its representation of the conflict over blood lines and continuity, the film addresses critically, if obliquely, growing ethnocentrism and nationalism in the US and abroad, translated into domestic and familial terms through the uses of biography.

. . . .

The writers of the *Queen Christina* screenplay derived the bare-bones biographical account of Christina of Sweden from Faith Compton Mackenzie's *The Sibyl of the North*, while Margaret Goldsmith provided a 'psychological' portrait of the queen in a book published in the year the film was made. These authors recount that Christina was the child of Swedish King Gustavus Adolphus and of a German

Lutheran princess, Marie Eleonore of Brandenburg. The king died at age thirty-eight on the battlefield at Lutzen during the Thirty Years War, leaving Christina as king under the regency of council and of Axel Oxenstierna in particular. (In Sweden the title of 'King' is reserved for the successor to the throne and ruler of the country, while a 'Queen' is merely the wife of a ruling monarch.) The child was left to cope with a petulant and semi-literate mother who disliked her. According to the decree of Gustavus, however, Christina received a masculine education. She was particularly drawn to scholarship and was a prodigious reader.

A sickly child and adult, Christina was not reputed to be beautiful, though she was described as attractive by those who enjoyed her erudite conversation. She horrified her attendants by her neglect of her appearance, and she was completely uninterested in feminine attire. As she grew older, the question of succession became a problem for her courtiers, but she had announced to one and all that she was determined never to marry. She preferred the company of Ebba Sparre, her lady-in-waiting, and she made clear her preferences more generally for other women.

Christina liked to surround herself with scientists and philosophers and was a patron of intellectual work. She was vehement in her hatred of warfare and continuously expressed democratic tendencies. She was a great admirer of continental thought (philosophers would have it that the cold Swedish winter killed Descartes, whom Christina had invited to her court), and she also exhibited a decided antipathy to Lutheranism which later resulted in her conversion to Roman Catholicism. Well before her abdication, she selected her cousin, Charles Augustus, as her heir and successor.

Christina was crowned in 1650 with an elaborate ceremony, but by the following year and after a severe illness, she made it clear that her intention was to abdicate. On recuperating from her illness, she spent an inordinate amount of time at balls and masquerades. At this time, the Spanish Ambassador, Don Antonio Pimentel, arrived at court and was reputed to be her lover, although he was not the first to share that honour. By 1653, facing a domestic crisis, Christina reiterated her resolve to abdicate, and by 1654 a financial settlement was arranged for her. She was a popular figure, and, on news of her abdication, she received petitions from the peasants to remain as ruling monarch.

The abdication ceremony was solemn. She was handed the symbols of power, which she then relinquished. Before an audience of courtiers, she read her declaration of abdication, releasing her subjects to Charles Augustus. She then gave thanks to God and exited. Three days after the abdication, dressed as a man and calling herself Count Dohna, she left Sweden forever; after a life of notoriety, she died in Rome in 1689.[38]

The elements of this narrative which have cinematic (and melodramatic) potential involve the familial conflict. The film transfers her maternal struggles to Christina's surrogate father, Count Axel Oxenstierna, regent and head of the Council. It is primarily with him that she battles about her marriage and about affairs of state, and it is to him that she lays her complaints about the stultifying nature of kingship. Christina's love affairs with both men and women provide meaty melodramatic material, as does the most dramatic event of her life, her abdication of the throne. The rituals of coronation and abdication offer opportunity for spectacle, replete with ornate costumes, symbols of power, elaborate choreography of the courtiers, and an aristocratic *mise en scène*. At the centre of the spectacle is a lone woman pitted against powerful men, a preoccupation heightened by Mamoulian's direction, particularly his operatic sense.

The choreography of these scenes in the Diet stresses the contrast between generation and gender, first through the child who plays the young Christina (Cora Sue Collins) and then through Garbo in her conflict with the masculine courtiers. In reading the various treatments until the final shooting script, one sees how melodrama and spectacle will compete with the outline of the biographical narrative. Whatever sources were used for the script, it is clear that what emerged was a compendium of these accounts, embellished by the requirements of the genre and by the actress who was to play the queen. Familiar with Christina's biography, Garbo leaned towards altering her appearance for the sake of realism by undergoing a nose job to imitate the queen's portrait. Of course, such a strategy was unacceptable to the studio.

Since Garbo's face was the signature of her films, the mark of the star, the *raison d'être* for the recreation of Christina's life, altering her appearance was unthinkable. But her willingness to change her appearance dramatically to suit the character offers another interesting insight into Garbo's dedication to her role as an actress in contrast to the studio's exploitation of her physiognomy. According to William Daniels, there was not one Garbo face, but many, as the wide variety of photographs of her amply illustrate. Even without the larger nose, Garbo, with the help of costume, lighting and her changing facial expressions, manages in the film to convey a range of nuanced responses. Significantly, her appearance shifts between a dignified plainness and extraordinary beauty, a trait attributed to Christina by her biographers. S. N. Behrman, who was one of the major architects of the dialogue for the film, described the 'quality of aristocracy' that Garbo brought to her performances as 'lambent' in *Queen Christina*. He added, 'I felt as I watched her that she is the most patrician artist in the world.'[39]

. . . .

Once the elements of the plot are laid bare in succession – Christina's coronation, conflict with her nobles, her romance with Don Antonio, opposition from her courtiers and from Don Antonio's rival, her abdication, the death of Don Antonio, and her departure from Sweden – the substance of the film resides in Garbo's reactions to these events. The visual power of *Queen Christina* derives in large measure from the spectacular nature of Garbo's face, which is highlighted in every conceivable manner to accentuate its contours. In the various stylised poses, with her head tilted upwards or to the side, her face appears to resemble an icon. Her physiognomy is more like a series of masks, or the white face of pantomime, than a human face, and her make-up enhances this effect.

Thanks to the orchestration of facial expression and gesture, memory of the final episode aboard ship lingers long after the film is gone, as does Christina's image in the bedroom scene with Don Antonio and in the night scenes with Oxenstierna prior to her abdication. According to Daniels, photographing Garbo's face was a matter of closeness and of lighting. Also, Mamoulian, in describing the last sequence aboard ship, recalled that he told Garbo, 'I want your face to be a blank sheet of paper. I want the writing to be done by everyone in the audience. I'd like it if you could avoid even blinking your eyes, so that you're nothing but a musical mask.'[40] This view of the filming is admittedly retrospective, but it does touch on an important dimension of the photography in the film, akin to the character of portraiture. Mamoulian's description of the masklike quality of the face has a parallel in the general treatment of the narrative, which is also highly stylised. Many of the most important sequences are designed as tableaux: the scenes in the Diet during the coronation and abdication, Christina's confrontation with Ebba Sparre and her fiancé as they stand on the stairs and Christina stands below them, and her confrontation with her disaffected subjects on the castle stairs as she stands above them. These scenes are in striking contrast to the more dynamic sense of the inn scenes.

The alternation between group scenes and isolated shots of Garbo enhances Garbo's character and her facial qualities. Gilles Deleuze's discussion of the nature of the close-up is helpful for finding a language that accounts for the uses of the face in cinema, especially Garbo's face. Deleuze finds that the close-up shifts between what he calls a reflecting close-up and an intensive close-up face. The reflecting face is one that projects thought. 'Mental reflection,' Deleuze writes, 'is undoubtedly the process by which one thinks of something. But it is cinematographically accompanied by a more radical reflection expressing a pure quality, which is common to several different things (the object which carries it, the body which submits to it, the idea which represents it, the face which has this idea).'[41] The intensive face in close-up, on the other hand, seems to convey affect rather than thought: the face of desire as opposed to wonder evident in the scenes of Christina with Ebba and with Don Antonio. Mamoulian's advice to Garbo to be blank to allow the audience to write on this face would seem to invite the spectator to read thought or affect into the face, shuttling between the poles Deleuze describes. Moreover, to obliterate any specificity of Garbo's image, he shot the scene with 'a soft-focusing lens to tone down close details', to present the face 'without lunar craters'.[42]

In Mamoulian's anecdote about his instructions for Garbo for the last shot, he understood how the face as mask allows the audience to write the meaning on the face themselves: '... no matter what feelings are portrayed by an actress, and these could range from hysterical sobs to a smile, some of the audience would disagree, find them wrong ... if the face is blank like John Locke's *tabula rasa*, then every member of the audience will inevitably write in his own emotions.'[43] Mamoulian's anecdote is a more pragmatic way of describing the potential of the face to communicate thought and feeling, to alternate between these poles, which may account for the film's appeal across widely differing audiences. In talking about the capacity of the face to express wonder, to give the illusion of having an idea, Deleuze also suggests that this is not a specific idea but a generalised sense. Mamoulian's description of the effects he desired seems consonant with the notion of producing a sense of pure quality. This quality of immobility and generality he deemed would be destroyed through dialogue and specific gestures.

But Garbo's face in other moments of the film – with Ebba, with Don Antonio, and in the inn scene – seems to convey another dimension of her persona, one that communicates passion and desire. The Garbo face moves between thought and passion, reflection and intensity, depending on the eyes, the lips, the tilt of the head, to provide an index to the quality of affect. Daniels tends to focus on Garbo's eyes, he tells us, to discover what she is thinking. The face reflects objects in the room, but it also looks at these objects and at other people. The heavy emphasis on the close-up also serves, as does the choreography, to isolate Garbo from others, emphasising her separateness in addition to conveying the desired affect of the scene.

While Garbo's face is the vortex into which the spectator falls, her voice is also important as an index to her regal star persona as well as to the regal persona of Christina. Her voice is low, husky, and occasionally her words are slurred, but not to the extent that they are incomprehensible. As she mouths the various characters' names, she intones her affective response to them. Parker Tyler commented on the distinctiveness of Garbo's voice: 'a bitter chocolate color and notes that fell securely into place as notes on a harp'.[44] This fortuitous combination of timbre, tone, accent and cadence contributed to Garbo's orchestrated performance. Tyler's comments underscore the musicality of her voice as suited to the melodramatic excess her persona enacts, thus reinforcing a further connection of Garbo with the opera diva. Not only is her voice a suitable vehicle for melodrama, especially pathos, but it complements the statuesque and stylised uses of her face and body.

There is also a certain breathlessness to her delivery. She seems to suck in certain sounds. Instead of a highly intense and fast flow of words, her presentation is understated, but this tendency does not minimise affect. Rather, the affect suggested is ambiguous, very much like her visual image, capable of being construed in several, often contradictory, ways. The slow and rhythmic pacing of her words and the cadences of her speech, while conveying a sense of melancholy, are also frequently conjoined with a particularly ironic and mocking tone. The film relies on the humour produced by ambiguity in Christina's interactions with Don Antonio; in the scene in which they first meet, when Christina rescues Don Antonio's coach from a snow bluff, her mocking tone undercuts the romantic suggestions of the sequence. Similarly, when Christina, masquerading as a common man, adjudicates between the soldiers' contentions about the number of lovers the queen is reputed to have had, she preserves the same ironic tone, converting suggestions of feminine promiscuity to playful conquest.

Garbo's movement in the film also becomes a significant carrier of affect. In describing the uses of her body, Charles Affron remarks on the contrasts in her pace, alternating between the forceful striding that characterises her movement in the palace and the Diet and the slow movement with which she memorises the objects during the inn scene. He writes: 'Striding with breathless rapidity through the throne room after the abdication, she is apt for state occasions and massed effects as for the languorous intimacies of the boudoir.'[45] Joseph I. Breen's insistence that Garbo be kept away from the bed acknowledges the sensuousness with which she places herself on the bed and caresses the pillow. There is a striking contrast established between her previous masculine posturing and her more intimate romantic scenes. The movement in the former is fast-paced and dynamic, the latter slow and deliberate: one energetic, the other elegiac.

The power of the bedroom scene is dependent on the orchestration of a number of details. First, in Garbo's slow movement around the room we catch only a brief glimpse of Don Antonio. The scene is hers alone. The lighting, which Daniels described as seeming to come from the fire but which was actually enhanced by small spotlights on the bedposts, highlights Garbo's image and fuses her with the objects she touches. Mamoulian described the desired effect of mingling sight and touch, conjoined with her graceful stopping and lingering before she moves to the next object, as an attempt to produce a lyrical effect akin to a sonnet. The reflection of Garbo's image in the mirror, doubling her presence, underscores her self-preoccupation.

Overleaf: Garbo and Gilbert in their bedroom scene

The sequence produces a reverse effect to the monumentalism often associated with the biopic that deals with political and royal subjects. Monumental treatments rely on architecture, portraiture, statuary and documents to reinforce the epic sweep of official history and the power of the state. By contrast, this scene reveals an intimacy that arises from the everyday and the familiar. Yet it is illuminating for the ways in which it offers clues to the functioning of memory in the film.

With each object Christina touches, one is strikingly aware of how the immediate present has become the past, just as her relations with Don Antonio have already become part of the past. What this scene offers through the self-conscious strategy of recollection is a melancholy perception of the passage of time. Garbo's fetishising of each object, and by extension of all objects, carries with it the reminder of its evanescence, of its presence and its looming absence. Gilles Deleuze, in his discussion of the time image, remarks in a complex passage:

> What is actual is always a present. But then, precisely, the present changes or passes. We can always say that it becomes past when it no longer is, when a new present replaces it. But this is meaningless. It is clearly necessary for it to pass at the same time as it is present, at the moment it is present. Thus the image has to be present and past, still present and already past, at one and the same time. . . . The past does not follow the present that it is no longer; it coexists with the present that was. The present is the actual image and *its* contemporaneous past is the virtual image, the image in a mirror.[46]

The memorability of Garbo's performance has thus to do with its preoccupation with the complexity of memory. Like Garbo's reflection in the mirror, the play on perception and recollection infuses the scene in the bedroom of the inn. The consciousness of the passage of time as Garbo moves from one object to another creates a tension between the actual image and its loss from sight, the coexistence of seeing and the passage of images from sight. The scene thus offers a metaphor for cinema, if not for experience more generally, and the force of its melancholy conception of time has captured generations of spectators. The scene also proposes a twist on monumental history through its merging of other aspects of recollection. The history of Queen Christina becomes present through the acting of Garbo, but only as an image that is virtual, to borrow Deleuze's language.

Again, in contrast to monumental history which creates a sense of the grandiosity of the past, this form of recollection modifies the past, subjecting past events and concepts of monumentality itself to a devolution, reducing the largeness of the past to its screen image and producing a meditation on the evanescent nature of memory and loss. This sequence, then, dramatises the mutability of time and the burdensome nature of power as duty and responsibility. It reinforces Christina's protests, in her speech to Oxenstierna, that she has become a symbol, drained of the capacity for human experience. The melodramatic rewriting of power as evanescent offered a provocative commentary on contemporary social relations in the context of the growing international conflicts in the interwar years, most notably the rise of fascism and the threat of war. This thematic did not pass unobserved, for as Salka Viertel noted, '*Queen Christina* was one of the last American films shown in the Third Reich. Friends and strangers wrote to me praising it for its pacifist tendency and abdication of power.'[47] This remark offers testimony to a recognition by spectators of the presence of contemporary popular history in film and of the reliance of melodrama on memory.

Similar conflicts regarding the nature of power shaped Garbo's Hollywood persona. A number of historical texts and loose associations forged through Hollywood folklore positioned her as a victim of power and unyielding forces: the frequent comparisons of Garbo with Eleonora Duse and Sarah Bernhardt, the image of her (at times ridiculed) of seeking to be alone, her virtual isolation in a foreign country, and her burden of fame (the flip side of the demand on her to sacrifice herself as a public property). These associations of Garbo with imprisonment, constraint and isolation inflect *Queen Christina* and sustain readings of the film which foreground the melodramatic thematic of power and victimisation, the tension between power and the desire to escape its demands. Garbo's persona was also distinctly androgynous; with Marlene Dietrich she introduced trousers for women to Hollywood, preferred flats to heels, and frequently referred to herself with masculine pronouns.[48]

The film aligns the question of power, the tension between

symbolic power and personal power, with the question of gender, the tension between masculinity and femininity, from its very first sequence, and it gains momentum through the cross-dressing sequence at the inn. Garbo's androgynous persona only serves to strengthen the identity between Garbo and the queen she plays. For Rebecca Bell-Metereau, that identity is most evident in components of Garbo's screen behaviour. 'All these elements are written into the script, but the rest of Garbo's masculinity resides in her herself – in the brusqueness of her movements, the long stride, the forceful hand gestures, the tone of her voice, and the angularity and big-boned quality of her frame.'[49]

What is interesting about *Queen Christina* is that it does not simply renounce symbolic power for personal power, nor does it propose an analogous renunciation of masculinity for femininity. It is difficult to agree with Bell-Metereau that the film presents a final image of domesticated femininity through a 'whitewashed' counterfactual historical account, 'maintaining the image of woman as essentially emotional, domestic, and without outside political or ethical concerns'.[50] This view slights the lingering power of the image of Garbo's strength not only at the end of the film but also in images preserved through spectators' memories, cherished as morsels of anti-hegemonic views of femininity. Jane Gaines takes this latter objection one step further, proposing that images of Garbo in drag, both literally in the scene involving her cross-dressing and more generally in images of the queen as 'masculine' early in the film, especially when she bestows her famous kiss on Ebba Sparre (Elizabeth Young), serve as special moments of pleasure for lesbian spectators (adding the dimension of sexuality to the analysis of power conflicts in the film). While this line of reasoning has tended to lead to speculations regarding Garbo's 'real' sexuality (is she or isn't she?) and to murky empirical investigations of 'real' lesbian spectators' reactions to the film, Gaines herself opens a rather different route for investigating the erotic dimensions of power in *Queen Christina* through an analysis of Adrian's costumes, an extremely important component of *mise en scène* in the film.

Gaines contends that Adrian's costumes function as an ironic, high-camp commentary on the constructed nature of power as it is represented in *Queen Christina*. Rather than seeing the masculine/

feminine duality as immutable and resolved on the unhappy side of
traditional femininity, Gaines proposes that Adrian's costumes reveal
the unstable nature of gender and sexual identity as such. By switching
between masculine and feminine modes, the costumes 'set up the
homosexual/heterosexual flip flop'[51] which demonstrates that each term
in the binary pairs – masculine/feminine, homosexual/heterosexual,
and symbolic/personal power – depends on the other for its mooring.
Moreover, the fluidity of these binary terms calls into question strict
binary notions of spectatorship designated along the masculine/
feminine axis. Gaines's essay is exemplary for its attempt to understand
the dialectical relation between narrative and spectacle, and for its
attention to hitherto invisible gay labour in Hollywood. An analysis of
the costumes in *Queen Christina* supports her argument and also reveals
how the costuming connects to other elements of the *mise en scène* and
to Garbo's persona.

Garbo's masculine costumes enable her to stride through the
palace, ride about the countryside, and move about freely. At times,
they also allow her to speak her mind without regard for 'proper' regal

behaviour: she denounces the brutal war, advocates peace, scholarship, and the 'arts of living'. These costumes signify leisure, mobility, freedom from constraint, and a form of pleasure that sits in marked contrast to her regal gowns. These sport stiff collars, as if serving her head upon a platter, and emphasise the weight of her royal role, especially in the instance of the ivory dress (encrusted with metallic thread and embedded with diamonds) and the heavy coronation robe in striking black and white. The stiff collars serve to call attention to her face as much as they de-eroticise her body, and the crown which accompanies them frames her face and guarantees its inaccessibility. In further contrast to these conspicuous emblems of state, Adrian designed clinging gowns and robes of silk and velvet, meant to signify Christina's femininity but also revealing femininity as (a) 'put on' in tension with a simplicity that characterises these costumes. Wide hats with tremendous plumage link the masculine and feminine guises of Christina: the hat, for example, that she wears at the end of the film with her velvet outfit appears to be a feminine version of her masculine attire.

While Garbo's clothing is appropriate for a seventeenth-century monarch, it was also at home in twentieth-century Hollywood and was exploited in the film's advertising campaign, as was Garbo's look more generally. The much imitated simplicity of Garbo's make-up and hair styles (true eyelashes, little shadow or eyeliner, little rouge, stark extended eyebrows, and a simple page boy haircut) allows the costumes to multiply the many images of Garbo. Several costumes in particular illustrate Garbo's movement between the opposing poles of past and present, masculine and feminine, power and abdication of power; it is the very indeterminacy of her place in relation to different characters and events that also complicates her position in the film and for her audiences.

The most unconstraining costume Garbo wears is the robe in the night throne room scene in which she struggles with Oxenstierna about her future. Her clothing is a correlative of her unsettled desires as she tells her councillor, 'I have been a symbol of eternal changelessness, an abstraction. A human being is mortal and changeable with desires and impurities, hopes and despairs. I'm tired of being a symbol, Chancellor. I long to be a human being, a longing I cannot suppress.' This scene seems designed more than others with the star image of Garbo in mind; at this moment, Christina becomes Garbo, and Garbo becomes the consummate incarnation of the diva. As the figure of excess, the diva thrives on pain, discomfort and a longing to be free; she articulates desire but, at every turn, finds that pleasure eludes her, or rather that the pleasure resides in the suffering. It is in the discontent with being a symbol that the extraordinary and the ordinary meet in the figure of the diva/star and in the figure here of Garbo. This discontent, arising from expectations on the part of others concerning her role, unifies the person Garbo with the star – as if the two were really inseparable – and also links the star to her audience since this dilemma is not unique to her but intrinsic to cultural conflicts concerning identity problems. Garbo's comments complicate the issue of authenticity, too, further exposing the tensions between representation and the desire for authenticity, actual and virtual memory, and questions relating to loss.

The gown that Christina wears in her abdication scene after her regal robe is removed resembles the robe she wears in the night throne room scene. It is white and flowing, tied loosely at the waist and lacks

46   At night in the throne room

the regal high starched collar. The gown now seems to represent the freedom that Christina has sought. She herself removes the heavy crown, the symbol of her monarchy. The scene foregrounds the issues of looking and of memory in her address to her subjects: 'Let me look at you once more. Let me remember you with love and loyalty until memory is no more.' The film again invokes memory as nostalgia, with its attendant pain, the '-*algia*' providing the index to Garbo's freedom in her need to freeze her gaze at objects to memorialise the past. At this point, other memories from within the film infuse Christina's need to remember – the death of her father-king, her own symbolic death, and an anticipation of Antonio's death – while the film itself is an exercise in cinematic memory.

The last outfit that Garbo wears in the film serves as an emblem of the various conflicts that remain unresolved on a narrative level but may be resolved in their irresolution. She wears a soft velvet outfit that appears to be a feminine version of her earlier masculine attire. The hat she wears is similar to the hat she donned with her earlier suits as well. Unlike the dress she wears at her abdication, which is white, this outfit

Abdication

is dark, though not black. Gone, too, are the stiff collars. The in-between nature of the garment seems to situate her in a place between masculine and feminine, homosexuality and heterosexuality, symbol and mortal, public and private person. Her arrival aboard ship to find Don Antonio dead at the hand of Magnus leaves her neither a king nor a lover.

As in the last act of a romantic opera, there is death and mourning; the death, however, is here not of the woman but of the man. After undergoing the act of mourning for the dead Antonio, Garbo embarks on the sea. She sits at the prow of the ship, standing before the wooden circular carving with the wind blowing at her hair. Her face and torso are prominently displayed, but the lower part of her body is hidden by the wood. Her image thus seems to be that of a figurehead, characteristic of earlier seafaring vessels, and while she may no longer be a symbol of state, she is nonetheless an icon of some indeterminate nature which provides uneasy closure.

The biopic, as a subgenre of the historical film, pays a great deal of attention to the *mise en scène* which, like the costumes, provides the historical ambience. There is, of course, great liberty taken with both to serve the interests of the narrative and particularly the expressive needs of melodrama. In *The Scarlet Empress* (the Sternberg/Dietrich melodrama of the same year as *Queen Christina*, about Catherine the Great), for example, icons and the grotesque statuary, as well as Byzantine turrets, function as much to communicate the despotism of the court and of Catherine's rise to power as they do to provide historical context. In *Queen Christina*, too, the exterior settings – the castle, the inn – convey the poles of Christina's dilemma between duty and freedom as much as they represent the 'authentic' historical setting of which the studio boasted in its advertising campaign. The massive walls and high ceilings of the castle, impressive formal achievements in the use of deep space, also function as metaphors for the resolute nature of state power.

Other aspects of the *mise en scène*, such as setting and figure positioning, reinforce the tensions between the symbolic and the personal modes of power, and between masculinity and femininity. With regard to setting, for example, paintings hang throughout the castle, but it is the portrait of Gustavus, like the presence of the actual king at the beginning of the film, that functions as a commentary on

The last outfit: unresolved masculinity/femininity

kingship and continuity, masculinity and patrilineage. The books on the shelves behind Christina's desk serve as indices to her scholarliness. The heavy and dark wooden carved furniture, echoed in the carved wooden wainscoting, seems to function as an unyielding point of reference symbolic of the unwavering world which she resists. Her movement through the palace appears to be against, rather than among, the objects within it. She is imprisoned behind her desk in her ornate chair as she greets the French ambassador, surrounded by her two mastiffs, and she is likewise imprisoned on her throne, the vastness of which is foregrounded in the opening sequence with the young Christina. As she moves through the palace, the shots of the corridors reinforce the sense of closed rather than open space associated with the palace, and in the night scene when she walks with her candles like a somnambulist to her throne, the surrounding darkness threatens to engulf her. In contrast to the forbidding and constraining interior settings of the palace, the inn appears bright and freshly painted, its rustic quality enhanced by the beer-guzzling convivial peasants inside.

With regard to figure positioning, Garbo's posture as a queen is

statuesque. She seems to tower over her subjects in the Diet thanks to an elevated dais. Her figure gains in stature from the distance placed between her and others, and she is often positioned in windows, doorways and on stairs to distinguish her from others. In scenes in which she encounters courtiers, she is set either spatially apart from them or above them. While the objects in the palace may surround her, other people rarely occupy the same space as Christina. Even in the scene at the tavern, when she is most at one with 'the people' in the crowded room, she stands on the table to quell the disorder sparked by an argument about the number of her lovers, and she is again spatially distinguished from the others. The bedroom sequence places her in close proximity to objects in the room, but here, by contrast, through her gaze and touch, she appears to fuse with them rather than be engulfed by them as she is in the castle.

The film also sets up a contrast between inside and outside, between nature and architecture. Among the many identifications of Christina with nature, the most famous is the morning scene when she steps out on the battlements and washes her face with snow. As Alexander Walker describes this scene, Garbo appears to give herself a 'brisk orgasmic face rub with a scooped up handful of snow'.[52] The cold snow furnishes Christina with pleasure, if not auto-erotic ecstasy, as she rides freely about her kingdom, and that pleasure stands again in contrast to the rigidity of the looming interiors of the palace. The snow also bogs down Don Antonio's carriage, serving as a foreshadowing of his unfortunate end in the cold regions of Sweden, and Christina's approach to the inn in the falling snow with her manservant, Aage, anticipates the lengthy conversation between Christina and Antonio on the merits of the south over the north. The final shots of the film again situate Christina in nature, aboard ship as the wind blows through her hair, a correlative (if an ironic one) for the freedom she has sought. The early versions of the script place this scene indoors, but the placement of the final action on the sea creates an ambiguity which undermines a reductive reading of the ending, suggesting either Christina's escape to freedom or the continuance of her isolation.

The music in *Queen Christina* provides structural support for those elements of *mise en scène* we have discussed: recitatives, costumes and setting as they are expressed in conventionalised conflicts involving the family, tragic misrecognitions, and duty both to nation and to loved ones. The melodrama thrives on its *melos*, which can arise from orchestral, violin or piano music, the scores of romantic composers – Tchaikovsky or Rachmaninoff in particular – but melodrama, or opera, is more than music. The film encodes these operatic concerns in its uses of spectacle, in Garbo as the consummate diva, and in conflicts between national duty and personal desire. The music for *Queen Christina* is outlined in a memo of 12 December 1933, and was mostly composed by Herbert Stothart, an MGM regular, as follows:

Reel 1 Opening – Prelude
    The Little Queen
    The Coronation
    The Ride
    Prince Charles
Reel 2 Peace Brings Dawn
Reel 3 The Snow Ride
Reel 4 To the Inn
Reel 5 To the Inn
Reel 6 Amour
    Serenata
    Coda Espagnole
    The Woman
Reel 7 Spanish Envoy
    Private Audience
Reel 8 Agitators
    The Mob
Reel 9 Night in the Throne Room
    Marche Regal
Reel 10 Engelbrekts Marschen (composer unknown)
Reel 11 Arrival at Dock
    Ship Sails

While the music is not distinctive, it serves to provide the appropriate ceremonial and melodramatic moments in the film. What is interesting about this listing is the way it reveals the tailoring of the music to specific scenes and to the film's dramatic requirements. The music, like the setting and the costuming, is not allowed to compete with the acting, especially Garbo's acting. In the early scenes with the child Christina, the music predictably enhances the courtly spectacle, culminating in the processional. The same can be said of the orchestral music which accompanies the victorious Prince Charles Augustus' progress to the throne to be greeted by his queen, repeated in Don Antonio's formal greeting later in the film. The riding music, also orchestral, punctuates the movement of the horses but does not provide any counterpoint which would undermine the sense of energy and forward movement conveyed in the sequence; it is timed to the quick hoof beats. The inn music similarly underscores the pacing; it is at first lively, as Christina enters the inn, and then becomes more lyrical, elegiac, as she moves about the room touching the various objects.

In the inn, the music further serves as a contrast to both the ceremonial music and the riding music. At the end of the film, the thematics of the slow and elegiac music seem to return us to the lyrical music of the more intimate scenes at the inn, establishing through a musical motif a connection between the thematic concerns of the two sequences: freedom, independence, loss, and memory. Similarly, the music that accompanies the night scene between Christina and Oxenstierna is slow and elegiac, beginning with violins. After the chancellor leaves, the music swells and fills in for the dialogue, offering an analogue, through its melancholy cast, to the queen's thought as she sits alone in the dark. While the music is therefore not innovative but typed to meet the demands of various scenes, to suit the desired mood, it is more than filler or ambience. Unlike the histrionic music of some melodramas, the music in *Queen Christina* is fused with the visual images, animating and enhancing the characters and events.

The *Queen Christina* overture

Unlike many melodramas, operas and historical films that rely on a reiterative theme, played in different registers throughout, the score to this film does not have recourse to theme and variations, except perhaps at the end with the echoed recapitulations of the earlier music. But the music generally seems designed to carry through the thematic contrasts between freedom and constraint, and it does so not only by punctuating significant thematic issues but also by heightening the film's play between sound and silence. While Christina is often verbal – in her several formal speeches, in her verbal challenges to her courtiers and chancellor, and in her repartee with Don Antonio and others – there is also a sense in which the film understands the importance, and significance, of silence. Garbo's awakening, her face-washing scene, her encounter with Ebba, as well as encounters between Christina and Don Antonio, are economical in terms of dialogue. The film's balancing of sound and silence is one aspect of its overall tight structure, achieved as well by the careful balancing of Garbo and the rest of the cast.

. . . .

While the image of its star dominates the film, *Queen Christina* is not all Garbo. Garbo's earlier relationship with John Gilbert had been highly publicised, and the publicity surrounding the film stresses the idea of Garbo and Gilbert 'together again'. That same rumour machine, however, had already marked Gilbert as a 'has been', a figure whose star was in a decline usually attributed to his inability to survive the transition to sound. The consensus now is that it was not Gilbert's voice that was not suited to sound film but that different factors contributed to his demise. Hedda Hopper commented that his persona as a great screen lover was undermined by 'a strange meeting that took place between his nose and his mouth which made him look more like a parrot than a lover. In silent films you never noticed.'[53] Others attribute Gilbert's failure to succeed in sound cinema to his antagonistic relations with Louis B. Mayer, as we have already noted. This was certainly Gilbert's view, and it is supported by others who claim that he was deliberately placed in pictures which did not feature him to advantage. Yet Samuel Marx concludes that 'audiences drew a cruel inference that if his voice sounded sissified, feminine tendencies must go with it.'[54] Hedda Hopper's comments, as well as Marx's, imply that

Gilbert's persona – whether because of temperament, physiognomy or voice – was dissonant with new expectations of masculinity on screen. Significantly, reviews of *Queen Christina*, while according glowing praise for Garbo 'and for the supporting cast, said nothing of Gilbert'.[55]

This critical neglect by the reviewers may be because Gilbert as Don Antonio clearly plays a subsidiary role in the film; in contrast to Garbo, his appearance is minimal. But that is only part of the story. There is an inequality in the acting as well as in the screen time allotted to Gilbert. Where Garbo's acting is redolent with complexity and ambiguity, Gilbert's appears to be merely bland. Charles Affron observes of most of Garbo's leading men that they 'mug and overplay' and notes in particular Gilbert's 'bug-eyed double take'[56] in the inn sequence. In contrast to Garbo's understated style, Gilbert does appear to overplay his reaction to the 'truth' of Christina's gender, while at other moments his acting is lifeless and wooden.

Gilbert's unsympathetic persona in *Queen Christina* is not due entirely to his acting but may also be attributable to the film's treatment of Don Antonio's masculinity, since the film seems to undermine any firm distinctions between masculinity and femininity in general. Certainly, from their first encounter in the snow, it is obvious that Christina has the upper hand over Don Antonio: her laughter at his predicament in a strange land and his ignorance about her identity cue the audience to Christina's narrative superiority and prepare them for further jokes at Don Antonio's expense. In the inn, Garbo's masquerade as a young man extends the joke perpetrated on the Spanish ambassador. As suggested earlier, the double entendres that arise out of their interaction, in which Christina plays on his ignorance of her gender and position, not only render him the butt of the joke but implicate him in this masquerade. The 'ambiguity' of Garbo's sexual identity, which fascinated critics link to her off-screen persona, extends in the bedroom sequence to Gilbert's on- and off-screen personae as well.

As we have indicated, the audience shares the knowledge that Christina is, after all, a woman, but what implications does this scene have for an understanding of Don Antonio's willingness to share the bed with another man? Exigency aside, his role skews conventional images of heterosexual masculinity, given innuendoes about his 'sissification' and his servant's reactions in the film. But even a queer reading which enjoys the suggestions of Gilbert's homosexuality in this sequence may miss the multiple playful layers of its joke: Garbo, in drag as a man (which delights many lesbian spectators), is offered the services of another woman (ditto pleasure) but sleeps with another man who is thereby implicated as gay. Surely the narrative is constructed so that the joke is on Gilbert, but it also does not require an identificatory reading position (a gay spectator, or a lesbian spectator) to 'get' it, and it may in fact discourage simple identifications in its narrative play.

The film also undermines Gilbert's persona through its characterisations of Don Antonio's foreignness in the Swedish court, in opposition to the fire-eating Magnus and Prince Palatine Charles. Resonances of the meaning of his foreign nature may be transposed from connotations of national identity to those of sexual identity. That he is slain by Magnus marks him further as a pathetic victim of court machinations rather than as a heroic figure. All this is not to say that he is unsatisfactory as a narrative figure playing against Garbo's queen, but instead to suggest that his role within the film works against his former intensely romantic silent screen image and against emerging notions of virility in the cinema.

The morning-after scene in the inn, in which Garbo and Gilbert speak of love, is significant too for the fact that their love-making scenes are remarkably chaste and devoid of erotic intensity. In fact, the covered bed shields the characters from the audience, preventing them from gaining any knowledge of what has transpired. Whether because of self-censorship, fear of the Hays Office, Garbo or Mamoulian, the audience is barred from any hint of the love-making, given only the sounds of Antonio's voice as his aide, Pedro, questions him about whether they will take chocolate. Thus it is left ambiguous whether anything actually transpired.

Is this scene an instance of the playing of another joke, this time not on Don Antonio but on the audience? Was the encounter between Garbo and Gilbert only an illusion? Garbo's following trance, committing the objects in the room to her memory with Gilbert as passive spectator to her movements, seems less to do with her love for the Spanish ambassador and her sensual attachment to him than with her self-absorption, her involvement in a performance that is decidedly different from her official role. Again, the camera isolates her from him: she does not finally share the scene with Gilbert. Her playful relationship to him appears instead to be one of camaraderie, not romance, and even in their costuming Garbo and Gilbert appear more similar than different.

While readings of the film stress the tragic ending, seeing Christina as 'a woman left with nothing – no kingdom, and no future but the pilgrimage to the land of her lost love', and as 'the masculine woman who is truly brave, gifted and iron willed ... beyond the comprehension of society or any one man',[57] an examination of the queen's relationship to Don Antonio would seem to suggest other possibilities. By scrutinising the film from a less moral and didactic position – and with a recognition of prevailing conflicts concerning genre and sexuality – one can see the film as challenging the very positions that the former reading wishes to solidify. The operatic spectacle, the play on memory, the reflexivity concerning cinematic illusion, and the spectacle of Garbo assume a complicity with audience knowledge about gender and sexual contradictions in the culture.

Like the game of hide and seek (now you see it, now you don't) between Garbo and Gilbert, which resonates with their past history and with conventional screen treatments of romance, *Queen Christina* plays a joke on both femininity and masculinity, working with and complicating the conventions associated with the biopic and with romance. This is not to argue that the film is a progressive text. But neither is it regressive. By acknowledging the complexities of the spectacle, one is able to move away from strictly narrative-driven analysis and its attempts to strap a text to a given set of meanings. The biopic then becomes a complicated set of representations, capable of generating affective relations which exceed the predictable and banal limits of textual analysis and interpretation. Too often critical assumptions that rely on monolithic ideological analysis misrepresent the contradictory and multi-faceted ways in which popular history in cinema is addressed to contemporary social constructions.

In contrast to Gilbert's and Garbo's unconventional roles – and to a lesser extent Elizabeth Young's as Ebba – the supporting cast for the film resembles the traditional types that inhabit the biopic and the historical romance. Lewis Stone was a regular in Garbo's films, and he admired her 'as an actress who stood alone. There was no one like her. She was Greta Garbo.'[58] Aside from his work with Garbo, Stone is best remembered now for his stern but genial portrayal of Judge Hardy in the later MGM Andy Hardy series, and his role as Axel Oxenstierna in *Queen Christina* is not dissimilar from that of the judge. As the foil against whom Garbo struggles to establish her freedom, Stone represents the conventional voice of continuity, duty and responsibility. A British actor, Reginald Owen, as Prince Palatine Charles Augustus, successor to the throne, plays a sturdy, blustering but not malicious man of action. Sir C. Aubrey Smith, who had worked with Mamoulian on *Love Me Tonight* (1932) and was to perform in the director's next film, *We Live Again* (1934), made his career as the perennial elder statesman, the high-ranking military figure, the wise grandfather and the professional upper-class Englishman. He deviates slightly in *Queen Christina* by playing a Swedish servant, but with his bushy eyebrows, his scowl, his common sense and his paternal attributes, he does not depart greatly from the qualities that were to carry over through his film career. Another British actor, Ian Keith as Magnus, is Don Antonio's nemesis, and his aggressiveness and militancy, his presence as a rabble-rousing irritant to Christina and his unwelcome advances to her establish him as the villain of the film, lacking in the integrity that characterises the other major courtiers.

These three roles, providing as they do the negative melodramatic pole to the narrative, serve as requisite opposition to Garbo. Her role and the issues engendered by it, however, exceed the narrative demands of the counterfoil. In fact, in most of the scenes in which she appears with these characters, the positioning of the characters reveals an inequality, both in the alternation between shots she shares with them and in those she occupies in isolation. Similarly, in the scenes in the Diet, the choreography functions to set her apart and often above them.

Elizabeth Young, a relative newcomer, plays her lady-in-waiting and the source of Garbo's disappointment. Her role is not the conventional confidante, since she is also the object of Christina's erotic attraction. In one respect, however, it is familiar in the royal biopic's narrative conventions: the young lady-in-waiting betrays the queen by falling in love with the queen's favourite, as in *Fire Over England* (1937) and *The Virgin Queen* (1955). The difference, of course, in *Queen Christina* resides in the queen's interest in the young woman and not the young man. Rumours of Garbo's off-screen dalliances with young starlets or with other members of her supporting casts bring additional resonances to Christina's infatuation with Ebba, and their famous kiss has been the subject of much attention over the years from lesbian spectators. Certainly, the inequality of power between the two women, the King/Queen and her servant, heightens the melodrama; as with national identity in the case of Don Antonio, here sexuality slides into the register of class, seeming to efface barriers to their mutual attraction.

The casting in general appears to favour age contrasts – the child queen and the mature Christina, the elderly Oxenstierna and the youthful Garbo as Christina, the old peasant and the younger queen, and the young queen and the seemingly more youthful Ebba. Other antitheses that are crucial to the narrative involve the opening scenes which portray the death of the old king, who says before he dies, 'I was King of Sweden.' This can be construed in retrospect as linked to Christina's abdication and to the last sequences in which that utterance applies to her as well. The literal death of Gustavus Adolphus is balanced against her symbolic death as King. The film, moreover,

Christina and Ebba Sparre

opens with one death and ends with another, Don Antonio's, which functions also as Christina's symbolic death. The film creates other balanced pairs: the coronation scene and the abdication scene (the crowning and its removal), the scenes of work and those of play, and the scenes at court and those at the inn. Just as Christina is positioned apart from her courtiers, she is also removed from the lower orders at the inn in her gentle rebuke to them.

Camera movement and positioning reinforce Christina's isolation from others, and the gentle zooms in and away from her face register her reactions to others, placing her at the centre of narrative knowledge and point of view. Striking long shots are reserved for the ceremonial scenes: the coronation of the child Christina, Christina's conflicts with her nobles in the parliament, and the abdication scene (which echoes the earlier ceremony). The film relies on a cinematographic motif to articulate the conflict between personal power and symbolic power, duty to state and personal freedom: when the camera moves towards Christina, the film tends to emphasise personal concerns, whereas the camera's tracking away from Christina inflects the monumental and regal aspects of her persona.

As we have suggested, however, the close-ups of Christina complicate the affective dimensions of the queen's (and Garbo's) image rather than solidifying a simple distinction between 'woman' and 'King'. Also, in the long shots of Christina at ceremonial occasions, the film offers more than a reified portrait of the queen performing her duties. These highly orchestrated shots are meant to reveal Christina's position among the other characters, arranged in almost rhythmic groups in the Diet, in which the patterned floors match the patterning of the actors. By contrast, the scenes at the inn are shot in middle distance when groups are shown, in medium close-up for Garbo with Gilbert set off from the others at a corner table. In this sequence, as with those involving the angry and discontented mobs, the chaotic sense distinguishes the narrative action at the inn from the orderly and constrained processes of court.

The play on looking in the film is similarly differentiated. The courtiers look at Christina, and she is an object of investigation for Oxenstierna (puzzled by her will and her malaise) and for Magnus (for whom she is both an erotic object and a subject for his control). To a lesser degree, Prince Charles looks at Christina, at times for her formal approval (as when he returns a war hero), but often subjecting her to a more disciplinary gaze. Don Antonio's looks seem less to be erotic gazes and more cues to the audience to follow Garbo's action, as in the bedroom sequence in the inn. Overriding the looks of the others, however, is Garbo's own Medusa-like gaze. Her glances at Magnus are imperious, those at Oxenstierna melancholic or ironic, and at Don Antonio amused, mocking and also ironic. Many of her glances, moreover, appear frontal rather than directly aligned to the characters who serve as their objects, as if she is looking beyond or through them; these help to designate a melodramatic 'beyond', a necessity for her tragic loneliness. When she looks at people or at objects, the look she projects is further one not of intimacy but of remoteness, which seems consonant with her line to Don Antonio, 'One can feel nostalgic for places one has never seen.'

Garbo's image produces a nostalgia for an image, especially her image. While the film sometimes calls attention to mirrors (Garbo's reflection, and the sequence involving her preparation for Don Antonio's formal reception), these shots are not excessive, since most

Christina orchestrated with her court

of the reflection in the film comes from Garbo's face directly to the spectator. The most self-conscious moment of the film in relation to spectatorship and the cinema, however, arises from Don Antonio's interrogation of Christina, who he fears may be an illusion and may disappear as an illusion does. His comment, like Garbo's attempt to absorb the objects in the bedroom through her touch and sight, serves as a metaphor for watching the film and for involvement with the star figure.

. . . .

If the closing sequence is intriguing as a meditation on the film's preoccupation with memory and history, the opening sequence plunges the spectator into the action of the film and establishes its central concerns. Mamoulian was known as a director whose opening scenes were designed to get things moving quickly and to anticipate the central structures of the narrative, and *Queen Christina*'s opening neatly establishes the trajectories of the conflicts to come. The sequence is brief in comparison to early versions of the script, which suggested a prolonged encounter between the king and his men, and, as Colonel Einhornung pointed out, skews historical 'fact' to present an older version of Gustavus. But in the context of the biopic, which subordinates its source material to thematic, melodramatic and spectacular elements, the aging of the king quickly introduces the thematic contrast in the film between temporality, aging and death, and the youth of the queen who is made to resemble a miniature Garbo. The emphasis on the symbolism of kingship and regal power subject to mortality provides the backdrop for Christina's later speech on mortality as the basis for her renunciation of power, her willingness to renounce the symbolic associated with her father and with the king's body.

The king's death is the prelude to the passing of this power to the new king, as it is in this case the suggestion of the continuity of the symbol of kingship. The opening, therefore, maps one of the film's trajectories concerning the relation of the symbolic to the masculine, and therefore of Christina's rejection of conventional concepts of masculinity. In other words, while the film indicates her preference for masculine attire and, early on, for other women, the film links masculinity unabashedly to war, death and hostile aggressivity and power. The introductory scene on the battlefield also establishes visual evidence for Christina's insistence on peace. The film thus opens a meditation on the social registers in which masculinity as such acquires meaning and force, but also seems to challenge attempts to define gender roles in isolation from other social relations, including the power of the state and ensuing racial conflicts.

Unlike *The Scarlet Empress*, the film has no need for elaborate titling to establish its concerns, a mark of the passing of the silent era techniques for providing context (although the film's acting still bears the imprint of silent film style). With the exception of the introductory title which frames the film's historical context (the location, year, monumental events), the actions and transitions in the rest of *Queen Christina* are sufficient in themselves. Also, with the exception of the close-up of the peace treaty signed by Christina, the film dispenses with images of maps, flags, treaties and the like often associated with historical films. The opening shot introduces, as synecdoche for state power, simply the emblems of state resting on a luxurious velvet pillow. The film, then, plunges into its narrative conflict by establishing

The child Queen (Cora Sue Collins) – a Garbo miniature

an enigma: the girl who was raised as a boy to fill the shoes of the dead Gustavus Adolphus. In visual answer to the peasant's demand, 'Let's see the child!', the film offers the miniature Garbo, the young Christina, but simultaneously denies the audience its look at the desired enigma, Garbo herself.

At her coronation, to be echoed and counterbalanced by her abdication, Christina enters in a processional and assumes the throne, in a shot from below the dais which underscores her power despite her youth and small size. Christina's independence is signified from the start as she refuses help in mounting the enormous throne, from which she then dismounts to make her first speech. In it, the young Christina takes her position on Sweden's participation in the Thirty Years War; faltering in this speech, in which she is meant to say (as Oxenstierna reminds her) that she promises that the Swedish army will 'wage it with courage', Christina substitutes a stronger claim, 'We promise to win it!' Out of the mouth of this young child, the promise seems both a reproach to Oxenstierna's weaker position (and she is thereby gendered as appropriately masculine for her place in the patriarchal descent of kings) but also barely believable. The older Christina will have to prove her credentials to utter such a promise of victory, central among them her successful assimilation into the masculine crafts of state associated with kingship.

Again the film answers its narrative question visually, through the following sequences of Christina on horseback in long shot and her entry into the palace, with dogs in tow, bounding up the massive stairway. The film withholds a close-up of Christina until we can bear it no longer, almost five and a half minutes after the opening credits. She meets her courtiers and chancellor to discuss the continuing war, and laments the loss of life and Sweden's resources in battle. The 'mature' Christina then changes the position which she had insisted upon in her youthful speech, especially concerning the problem of sacrificing the lives of Sweden's peasants to the cause. Her new proclamation, a demand for immediate peace, is therefore understood as empathetic, anti-war, respectful of the sacrifices of the people, a position consonant perhaps not only with a 1930s audience mindful of the tragedies of the First World War and not yet anticipating the Second, but also with cultural feminist identities between 'women' and 'peace', often grounded in a discourse of maternity.

Christina's position on peace is not, however, easily identifiable with women but is one that is embedded in and produced through a variety of other discourses, including but not limited to the maternal. Maternity itself is demanded of the monarch in the necessity of an heir to the throne, an heir Christina will not produce through marriage to her heroic cousin, Prince Charles. The film offers Christina's opposition to this coupling on two registers: her aversion to marriage in general ('I shall die a bachelor'), linked to her preference for Ebba Sparre, and her apparent love for Antonio. In the first case, Christina is seen as wilful and independent, not asexual or strictly lesbian as demonstrated in her liaison with Count Magnus. In the second, the film extends her independence to matters of choice regarding her mate and to conflicts between northern, Nordic rigidity and southern passion.

What the film ultimately presents, however, is the impossibility of Christina acting as sovereign and as wife at the same time, in other words, the complete incommensurability of these positions. The film never suggests that Christina was not a fine king, loved by the people and good to them, but it does construct the requirement to produce an heir as a demand of the position she cannot, or will not, fulfil. Maternity is not therefore posited as outside the position of king but as internal to its system, and Christina is somehow flawed in her inability to act as both king *and* queen by not rising to meet it. Her aversion to marriage could thus be read not just as a repudiation of one side of her 'nature' (the personal) in favour of state duties, nor as dogmatism in which she holds out for 'true love' with Antonio, nor even as 'true' lesbianism which refuses to be coded and glorified as heterosexual love, but rather as a statement about the impossibility of charting a position of motherhood and sexuality in the face of the state's contradiction between 'woman' and king. This reading of *Queen Christina* therefore sees Christina as providing an internal critique to the functioning of state roles and works against the type of reading which sees her desire, particularly lesbian desire, as outside, unrepresentable, 'ghosted' (to borrow Terry Castle's term) in a domain only decodable by bona fide lesbians.[59]

The film represents Christina as contesting the requirements of statehood in the second register in which we can read her aversion to marriage, whereupon it builds its condemnation of racism: her 'true love' for Antonio. In the film, 'true love' is not a personal, individualised narrative but rather always sits in relation to the views of the masses who monitor Christina's behaviour. The masses are aligned with the interests of state in so far as they demand an heir to the throne, and this is the motivating force behind their rejection of the 'foreigner' (swarthy Spaniard) Antonio who, with Christina, will not beget a full-blooded Swede. But Christina, through the sheer force of her personality, is able to command the masses' respect for her private affairs, appealing as she does to her right and training by descent to reign as king.

Pacified and re-enlisted as Christina's devotees, the masses disperse, only to be further goaded into disdain for Antonio by his rival for Christina's affections, Count Magnus. That rivalry is melodramatic, in so far as it creates a heightened sense of emotion, played out in the polar duel motivated by issues of propriety, appropriate familial constellations, and other stuff of which melodrama is made. The gossip which results in Antonio's trip outside Sweden, in Christina's abdication and in Antonio's death is shown to be an effective force in mobilising the masses on the issue of race, straining their loyalty to the individual monarch. The racist response to Antonio is grounded in 'biology', in that biology is the realm through which to preserve the purity of Swedish noble blood, which seems to act as a 'bedrock' determination of propriety. According to this logic, there is no way for Antonio to become a proper partner for Christina; there is no proper name for the place he would occupy (Queen to Christina's King?).

Within the limits of the masses' response, which echoes the limits of action in the face of memory, loss and desire, Christina can do nothing but abdicate, leaving for the coast of Antonio's Spain, an unknown realm which stands in for a tolerance and freedom from particular social constraints contrary to usual notions of Spain as feudal, hierarchical and repressive. The film derives its power, however, from denying Christina's union with Don Antonio and withholding a representation of a realm unaffected by the social forces with which she has struggled in Sweden. It therefore problematises the social construction of racism while at the same time introducing the dangers of discourses of biological purity. And it is the determination of the impossibility of Christina and Antonio's love in their biological incommensurability which makes the substitution of racism by homophobia (that reading which relies on an idea of homosexuality as the coupling of same-sexed bodies) possible in 'queer' readings of the film.

But that racism, in the end, is shown to be the position of only a vicious few: the masses love Christina, as do the members of her court, and they beg her to stay on. The film ultimately makes a bid for tolerance, for reducing antagonism and conflict, for preserving stability and order. And even though Christina will not accept those terms, choosing to leave despite Antonio's death, the film posits no resolution of the conflicts which drive her away. Hence the ambiguity of the final shot; if it is read in line with the tracking motif we discussed earlier, the camera tracking towards the face would seem to emphasise Christina's prolonged status as woman as opposed to queen; but she is not only encumbered by the constraints of public life (from which the personal is not severable) but also determined by the histories the film has traced. This reading stands against a more utopian stance, in which Christina is released into a world that makes no demands of her, where she can simply 'be' the woman she has dreamt of being throughout the film, although not resting 'in a man's arms'.

The final shot holds resolutely on to the film's struggles with gender and sexual conflicts that surround the issue of her refusal to marry and Oxenstierna's insistence that she do so. Thanks to Salka Viertel and S. N. Behrman, the film had prepared through its dialogue the thematic threads which the ending refuses to resolve. In its allusions to Molière, Calderón and Velazquez, the dialogue dramatises Christina's erudition and penchant for continental culture as opposed to the ethnocentrism of her courtiers. Her refusal to marry, and her disgust at having to sleep with a man, also allude to cosmopolitan and bohemian European culture as opposed to the constraints (or surface representations) of heterosexual star culture. Perhaps here, too, is embedded a familiar disdain for Americanism on the part of European émigrés such as Viertel and Garbo herself, particularly in its ethnocentrism and anti-intellectualism.

Similarly, the brief scene with the Archbishop concerning Uppsala University also extends beyond Christina's concern for education. There, too, she attacks the narrowness, the anti-European attitudes of Swedish intellectuals. She speaks on behalf of change and intermixing as she tells him, 'We need new wine in old bottles.' Here again, the contrast between youth and old age, the new and the old, comes into play. With Oxenstierna, as well, she will wax eloquent on the importance of philosophy and art, consistent with Mamoulian's own beliefs about their liberating force. Is it possible that the writers have also planted a critique of Hollywood, a critique that was on the lips of disenchanted intellectuals in the 1930s?

Thus Garbo/Christina comes to represent internationalism, intellectualism, anti-monarchical attitudes, and negative attitudes towards marriage and conventional behaviour as her role is written into the film, if not in the larger context of her star persona. The free-spirited image of the star and queen says nothing about the settlement on the queen that enabled her to live independently in Europe until her death, any more than it overtly weighs Garbo's image in terms of its economic value in dollars and cents, though her question to Oxenstierna – 'Must I smile for the masses?' – suggests some obligation of reciprocity beyond the idealism of service. This line, while seeking to account for Christina's disaffection with her royal role, carried the double meaning of the weight of Garbo's obligations as a studio property obliged to make public appearances by her employers at MGM and by the expectations of her fans. Thus the images of Queen Garbo and Queen Christina again merge.

After this film, Garbo would make only six more films for MGM and for Hollywood. John Gilbert would be dead in three years. Mamoulian would go on to make a number of melodramas, musicals, a fight film, and even a Western. C. Aubrey Smith and Reginald Owen would make careers as professional Englishmen. Irving Thalberg, the boy wonder of MGM, would be dead, and the films of MGM, in Thomas Schatz's terms, 'themselves become more conventional, and innovation was implicitly discouraged'.[60] *Queen Christina*, like most of Garbo's films, would stand as a testimonial to the passing of MGM's 'golden age'.

. . . .

Queen Christina is a film with which the image of Greta Garbo is most intimately fused, and not surprisingly, for the biopic is a conduit for the merging of historical narratives with star history through its fascination with the exceptional or exemplary figure. In the 1930s, biopics featuring the public and private lives of monarchs flourished; Alexander Korda's *The Private Life of Henry VIII* (1933) is considered the seminal film that encouraged other British and American producers, eager to imitate success, to emulate this mode of film-making. Concomitantly, by the 1930s too, Hollywood had solidified its strategy, within the studio system, for producing, circulating and managing its own royalty, specifically the movie queen. The fusion of historical narratives with star history in the biopic is not retrospective or accidental but was integral to the genre's promotion and popularity. Indeed, Metro-Goldwyn-Mayer's own promotional packet, including 'catchliners', for *Queen Christina* exploited the slippage between the movie queen and the historical queen: 'Sweden's most famous modern woman ... Garbo ... In the role of Sweden's historical courtesan queen of the past!'

The reception of *Queen Christina*, too, both at the time of its release and in the ensuing decades, has focused on the persona of Garbo as Queen Christina, foregrounding the difficulty, if not impossibility, of separating star images from the narratives in which they circulate. As a complex repository of biography, popular European history, star history, Hollywood history and folklore (including rumour and gossip) around royalty and its star, *Queen Christina* is exemplary of the myriad ways in which the biopic appropriates history, as well as for understanding how Hollywood, through the biopic, constructs and disseminates conceptions of sexuality, gender, national identity and power.

These densely woven layers of history sedimented in the biopic generally escape critical attention. With few exceptions, critics and reviewers scoff at the genre as unhistorical, citing the casual, sloppy ways in which the films adhere to written or official history; by relegating the films to the realm of fantasy, they neglect an opportunity for rethinking how popular history is created and disseminated. A rigid conception of what counts as history underwrites the overwhelming dismissal of the biopic. Official history, usually in the form of written accounts of monumental historical figures, takes critical precedence over popular memory, and biopics therefore fail the litmus test of historical 'accuracy' in their representations of the past, which tend in contrast to rely upon or invoke popular memory.

Since cinema as visual history is an amalgam of narrative and spectacle, critics valorise the former over the latter, which is the element of the biopic most often slighted as being unhistorical. If these rigid views of history efface the multivalent forms of historicising in the biopic, an understanding of the biopic as a compendium of official history, popular memory and folklore (around historical figures and stars themselves) can disclose the ways in which both the narrative and spectacular dimensions of cinema are carriers of important values and attitudes of historical representation. The realms of folklore and popular memory further reveal the significant slips, gaps and dislocations through which versions of the past are superimposed onto the present.

Films that feature queens (*Catherine the Great*, 1933; *The Scarlet Empress*, 1933; *Mary of Scotland*, 1936; *Tudor Rose*, 1936; and *Queen Christina*) are not only windows to Hollywood's and Britain's role in the developing consumer culture of the 1930s but also to the ways the exceptional woman becomes a vehicle for representations of popular history. The female biopic as a genre (or subgenre of the biopic centring on the monarch) bears some resemblance to the woman's film of the 1940s. As with the woman's film (a designation which describes both the narrative focus and the intended audience), the biopic narratives are woman-centred, relying on popular female stars (Marlene Dietrich, Bette Davis, Garbo) who dominate them. Generally, the male actors are lesser stars, and the roles they play within the narrative are subordinated to the problems of the star persona, who struggles in a conflict between power and personal desire. In the biopic, that struggle assumes a conflict, in *Queen Christina* a choice, between duty to the state and romance, between femininity and its renunciation. If the film pursues the latter course – and this is the more familiar form – and the dominant female figure renounces romance, then the narrative assumes the trajectory of an initiation, often painful and bitter, into responsibility.

What is intriguing about *Queen Christina* is not only its adherence to this narrative but the ways in which, building on knowledge of the genre, it diverges from it. Instead of the queen rejected in love and forced to accommodate a repulsive marriage of convenience, to resign herself to a lonely life of statecraft, *Queen Christina* offers a narrative of a queen renouncing her royal prerogatives for love. Her abdication of the throne of Sweden, in fact, is as important to the narrative as her relationship to her lover, Don Antonio, and the motives presented for her abdication exceed the romantic narrative. Elements belonging to the realm of the spectacular (costuming, music, *mise en scène*, cinematography) reveal the modalities of this excess and its links to *Queen Christina*'s representations of popular history in relation to sexuality, gender, and other power relations – nationalism and ethnocentrism.

The factors which contribute to the film's differences from other royal female biopics are intimately tied to the star figure of Garbo, and in particular to the ways in which MGM's personnel along with Garbo herself constructed images of the 'queen of Hollywood'. Neither the studio nor the figure of Garbo, however, can be taken as a simple, self-evident and independent entity; the publicity machines of Hollywood could not function without the studio system, and the studio system could not operate without tentacles that stretched into the culture at large. Conflicts within the studios regarding chains of power and control, the relation of studios to stars (and stars to them), and the types of films produced within the studios during the 1930s can be traced to Hollywood's sensitivity to the effects of the Depression and to changing social, moral and economic priorities during this turbulent decade. The star, then, did not exercise complete control over her image or her roles, but was rather the creation of a variety of determinants within the studio system and its parasites, the machines of rumour and gossip which daily spewed and revised chunks of biographical detail to support and contest the studios' versions of royal personae.

During her lifetime and since her death in 1990, Garbo has been celebrated above all as a figure of mystery. An elusive and reclusive star, during her film career as well as after her retirement from the screen in 1941 following *Two-Faced Woman*, she sparked the prurience of fans, critics and reviewers keen to condense her life and habits into a coherent story. Rilla Page Palmborg's 1931 biography of Garbo is typical in its introduction: 'No picture star in the world has aroused the curiosity about her private life that Greta Garbo has. No picture star in the world but Greta Garbo has been able to keep her private life so nearly a closed book.'[61] Of course, each biography promises to reveal the 'real Garbo', to disclose the secret, to resolve the contradiction of

Garbo's screen image and 'true self'. In Palmborg's words: 'The real Garbo and the femininely alluring Garbo of the screen are two distinct personalities.'[62]

In the main, these narratives of Garbo's life redirect a fascination with her prismatic and resonant image into a preoccupation with her indeterminate gender identity (the androgynous elements of her image and screen roles) and her ambiguous sexuality (the components of her star image that seduce both male and female spectators and the 'evidence' of her bisexuality or lesbian inclinations). The overarching biographical questions which motivate this line of enquiry –'is she or isn't she?' – tend to obscure other important considerations, namely the mechanisms through which her star image was produced, maintained, solidified, disputed. While the ambiguous and tantalising aspects of Garbo's gender and sexual significations are crucial to understanding *Queen Christina*, the text, like the figure of Garbo herself, was the consummate product of economic and cultural determinations in the 1930s mode of studio production. These cultural determinants were tied to the power of melodrama as the vehicle par excellence of elegiac affect. The affect is animated by a reverence and nostalgia for the past and a desire for a stable sense of sexual, gendered and national identity; it is also generated by the constraints of history and of identity. Like the opera diva, the star is the embodiment of this affect.

If *Queen Christina* gestures towards meditations on the evanescent nature of Garbo's beauty as subject to time, aging and death, this is because the film touches on the deepest chords of melodrama's operatic nature: the failure of verbal language, the fascination with *ars moriendi*, the art of dying well, and the diva as the supreme melodramatic agent. As we have suggested in discussing Garbo's gaze, the sights and sounds of the film point the way but can only suggest the most extreme melancholy and elegiac affect. This domain is that of the diva, the supreme instance of suffering mortality doomed to isolation and death. The particular conjunction of Garbo, whose beauty was linked to notions of royalty and divinity (the 'Divine Garbo'), with the figure of Queen Christina, who divests herself of the trappings of royalty, serves as a vehicle for the star. Since the accounts of Christina's abdication must always be subject to a certain conjecture, the film provides its own historical interpretation re-enacted through the image of the star. Stardom is intimately intertwined with the narratives enacted by stars; in other words, stardom is less a mystery than it is a cultural construction that feeds off memory and popular history.

The biopic is linked to other genres, to other forms of representing history, to existing forms of the 'melodramatic imagination', to borrow Peter Brooks' title. These, in turn, are dependent upon prevailing cultural dispositions towards regarding history in melodramatic fashion and circulating it through key personalities. In this case, Garbo, the star, is the instrument through which these conceptions of history circulate. As Andrew Britton writes, 'The star in his/her films must always be read as a dramatic presence which is predicated by, and which intervenes in, enormously complex and elaborate themes and motifs and thereby refers us to a particular state of the social reality of genre, and the relation among genres.'[63]

Stardom is therefore not the starting point to address this question of biopics, nor is the biopic the starting point to probe the nature of stardom. The dimensions of stardom which reach into Hollywood history, conjoined to the Hollywood uses of historical subjects, are multi-layered, reaching into the culture. And while this culture involves the industrial modes of production which characterise Hollywood, it also entails the circulation of historical narratives through all the tentacles of cultural production: education, religion, media, literature, music. Hollywood may have created stars, but before them were the biographical subjects which are the forms which Hollywood has superimposed onto the celluloid images. *Queen Christina*, then, is a prime instance of how the uses of history are intrinsic to popular culture though variable in treatment, depending upon the scenarios and upon those called to enact, or even embody, the subjects.

Thus, despite numerous studies to the contrary, and despite Antonio's line to Garbo in the film, 'There is a mystery to you', the film offers only the appearance of mystery. The apparent mystery is the 'coincidence', which is not a coincidence at all, of Garbo and the Swedish queen, as if this conjunction were not selected and painstakingly constructed (while at the same time, as we have seen, the film is concomitantly indebted to re-creation and repetition). The 'mystery' also resides in the celebration of Garbo's beauty, as if the culture did not construct its own standards of beauty. In every way imaginable – through photography, lighting, positioning of the star figure, and costuming – the mystery of the intrinsic nature of beauty is exploded as a sham. The 'mystery' may further appear to dwell in the contradictions between the exceptional nature of the individual and the commonality of social and physical conflicts. On the one hand, the exceptional figure personified by Garbo appears to function in a realm apart from commonplace mortality, and, on the other, she also seems to share that mortality with her audiences.

There is, to put it baldly, no mystery, no essential and determined quality to the protagonists of the biopic. Beauty is constructed around certain standards of Nordic fairness, youth, freedom from disfigurement, and statuesque bearing aided by the appurtenances of cinematic recording. Furthermore, where melodrama may seem to represent yet another permutation of the 'mystery' of life, the film exposes these conflicts as generated from contradictions involving social and political power and personal desire, and reveals that these contradictions are rendered 'ineffable' by linking their irreconcilability to the melancholy prospect of passing time, death and isolation. If there is no mystery, however, what interests are served by the continued insistence on it? On the one hand, the continued argument that there is something intrinsic, mysterious and absolute in Garbo's 'beauty' effaces or conceals the fabrication of her star image by industrial Hollywood.[64] But it is not enough to dismiss thereby the standards of beauty created through Hollywood images and narratives. Rather, as we have shown, star images elicit affective responses which strike powerful chords in spectators across a range of social/sexual positions, and it seems necessary to account for the relations between affective response and social conditions in their contradictions.

What seems most contradictory yet intriguing about the film's ending is that while Garbo as Christina had longed to be a person and not a symbol, the image of Garbo aboard the ship seems engineered to represent her as an artefact. The power of the shot derives from its reflexivity. In it, we become aware of Garbo *as* Garbo, of Queen Christina as Garbo and not the reverse. Garbo's look in the shot is off screen, but she is placed before us, the audience, as an object for contemplation. Mamoulian's familiar injunction for Garbo to remain blank, moreover, offers itself as a means for understanding stardom –

and exceptionality more generally – on a pragmatic as well as an analytical level. The star is the *tabula rasa* to which he refers, and the culture assigns it a value. There is no intrinsic value to Garbo or to Queen Christina; it has remained for the culture to create, legitimise and perpetuate the value of these 'exceptional' figures. Thus Mamoulian's instruction to remain blank seems an acknowledgment of the star's image as a blank cheque which must be signed by the producers and the spectators. It is also appropriate that the last sequence was filmed without dialogue, as if the dialogue would have detracted from the audience's affective involvement in Garbo's cinematic image, which, as Mamoulian understood in commonsense terms, could generate a number of different emotional responses (although the matrix for understanding the image is predetermined by Don Antonio's death, Christina's presumed loss, and familiarity with the Garbo image).

....

Queen Christina provides significant clues to Garbo's image, contributing new insights into how Garbo continues to signify as a star and more generally into how stardom is created. Michaela Krutzen's assertion that Garbo is frozen in history, and hence that her star image does not serve a dynamic role in contemporary culture, does not accord with our perceptions.[65] While the institution of stardom has certainly changed since the 1930s, revealing evolution in ideals of beauty and desirability, Garbo's films continue to circulate, and Garbo's persona is inextricable from the narratives in which she appeared. Garbo lives on, as legend, as biographical subject, as object of fascination for her fans, and testimony to unresolved questions concerning national, gendered and sexual representations – but through her

films, especially *Queen Christina*. Given the carefully guarded information about her life, her legend has been constructed from innuendo, rumour and gossip, but in her case, more than for most other stars, through the film texts themselves and the ways they have been appropriated. If *Queen Christina* is a 'classic', it is not because it follows certain formal rules of composition. It is not because the film is a memorial to the 'golden years' of MGM. It is not because it is 'universal', 'defying history'. Nor is it a 'classic' because the discipline of film study has rivalled other disciplines such as literature and painting in instituting a 'canon'. Nor, finally, is it a 'classic' because it bears Garbo's signature.

If the language of canon-formation is to be used, then *Queen Christina* is a classic because, as a product of popular culture and as a carrier of popular history, it continues to circulate knowledge in the US and internationally about cultural formations – about sexuality, familial relations, and the uses of memory. Garbo's image from *Queen Christina* circulates particularly as a 'camp' commodity or icon of lesbian stardom and as a signifier of unresolved (and contradictory) conflicts concerning femininity and masculinity. The film continues via television showings, video sales and rentals, posters, and academic commentaries like ours to highlight the central preoccupation with representation – the power of representation and representations of power.

NOTES

. . . .

1 Alexander Walker, *Garbo* (London:
Weidenfeld & Nicolson; New York:
Macmillan, 1980), pp. 132–3.
2 Betsy Erkkila, 'Greta Garbo: Sailing
Beyond the Frame', *Critical Inquiry* (June
1985), pp. 602–3.
3 Tom Milne, *Rouben Mamoulian* (London:
Thames and Hudson/BFI; Bloomington:
Indiana University Press, 1969), p. 7.
4 Andrew Sarris, *Interviews with Film
Directors* (New York: Avon, 1967), p. 345.
5 Milne, *Rouben Mamoulian*, p. 11.
6 Mark Spergel chronicles Mamoulian's
conception of the role of the director in his
recent biography, *Reinventing Reality: The
Art and Life of Rouben Mamoulian*
(Metuchen, NJ: Scarecrow Press, 1993),
especially pp. 13 and 150.
7 Ibid, p. 5.
8 Sheridan Morley, *Tales from the
Hollywood Raj: The British, the Movies, and
Tinseltown* (London: Weidenfeld &
Nicolson; New York: Viking, 1983), p. 89.
9 Leatrice Joy Fountain with John R.
Maxim, *Dark Star: The Untold Story of the
Meteoric Rise and Fall of the Legendary John
Gilbert* (New York: St Martin's Press, 1985).
10 Thomas Schatz, *The Genius of the
System: Hollywood Filmmaking in the Studio
Era* (New York: Pantheon, 1988), pp.
98–125.
11 William Daniels interview with Hedda
Hopper, in Hedda Hopper file, Academy of
Motion Picture Arts and Sciences, n.d.
12 William Daniels in Charles Higham
Hollywood Cameramen (London: Thames
and Hudson/BFI; Bloomington: Indiana
University Press, 1970), p. 70.
13 Daniels in *Hollywood Cameramen*, p. 72.
14 Clarence Bull, Hedda Hopper file.
15 Adrian, 'Adrian Answers 20 Questions
on Garbo', *The Talkies: Articles and
Illustrations from Photoplay Magazine
1928–1940*, Text and Arrangement by
Richard Griffith, Foreword by Lawrence J.
Quirk, (New York: Dover, 1971), p. 272.

16 Ibid.
17 Hedda Hopper, *From Under My Hat*
(Garden City, NY: Doubleday, 1952), p.
212.
18 Jane Gaines, 'The *Queen Christina* Tie-
Ups: Convergence of Shop Window and
Screen', *Quarterly Review of Film and Video*,
vol. II, pp. 35–60.
19 Salka Viertel, *The Kindness of Strangers*
(New York: Holt, Rinehart and Winston,
1969), pp. 152, 169.
20 Mr Feyder, 'Reader's Report', Academy
of Motion Picture Arts and Sciences file on
Queen Christina, 1932.
21 Jessie Burns, 'Reader's Report', ibid.,
2 May 1932.
22 Jessie Burns, 'Reader's Report', ibid.,
28 July 1932.
23 Salka Viertel and Margaret LeVino,
Queen Christina script, 15 August 1932,
Academy of Motion Picture Arts and
Sciences.
24 Bess Meredyth, Continuity, ibid.
25 Frederick Sands and Sven Broman,
Divine Garbo (New York: Grosset and
Dunlap, 1979), p. 117.
26 Walker, *Garbo*, p. 142.
27 George Macdonald Fraser, *The
Hollywood History of the World* (London:
Michael Joseph, 1989), p. 110.
28 Campaign Exhibitors Book, Academy of
Motion Pictures and Sciences.
29 *American Film Institute Catalogue of
Motion Pictures Produced in the United
States: Feature Films 1931–1940* (Berkeley:
University of California Press, 1988), p. 3.
30 Letter of James Wingate to E. J.
Mannix, 7 August 1933, *Queen Christina* file,
Academy of Motion Picture Arts and
Sciences.
31 Erkilla, 'Greta Garbo', p. 605.
32 Sarris, *Interviews with Film Directors*,
p. 346.

33 Ibid, p. 348.

34 Peter Brooks, *The Melodramatic Imagination: Balzac, Henry James, Melodrama, and the Mode of Excess* (New York: Columbia University Press, 1985), p. 56. See also Christine Gledhill, 'The Melodramatic Field: An Investigation', in *Home is Where the Heart Is* (London: BFI Publishing, 1987), pp. 5–39.

35 Christian Viviani, 'Who is Without Sin?: The Maternal Melodrama in American Film, 1930–1939', in *Home is Where the Heart Is*, p. 85.

36 MGM Ledger, Academy of Motion Picture Arts and Sciences. See also Samuel Marx, *The Make Believe Saints* (Hollywood, CA: Samuel French, 1988), pp. 260–1.

37 *The Talkies*, p. 11.

38 Margaret Goldsmith, *Christina of Sweden: A Psychological Biography* (Garden City, NY: Doubleday, Doran &Company, 1933).

39 S. N. Behrman, *People in a Diary: A Memoir* (Boston, MA: Little, Brown and Company, 1972), p. 151.

40 Milne, *Rouben Mamoulian*, pp. 74–5.

41 Gilles Deleuze, *Cinema 1: The Movement Image* (Minneapolis: University of Minnesota Press, 1986), p. 90.

42 Michaela Krutzen, *The Most Beautiful Woman on the Screen: The Fabrication of Greta Garbo* (Frankfurt am Main: Peter Lang, 1992), p. 21.

43 Sarris, *Interviews with Film Directors*, p. 348.

44 Parker Tyler, *Magic and Myth of the Movies* (New York: Simon and Schuster, 1970), p. 7.

45 Charles Affron, *Cinema and Sentiment* (Chicago: University of Chicago Press, 1982), p. 179.

46 Gilles Deleuze, *Cinema 2: The Time Image* (Minneapolis: University of Minnesota Press, 1989), pp. 78–9.

47 Viertel, *The Kindness of Strangers*, p. 197.

48 Barry Paris, *Garbo* (New York: Alfred Knopf, 1995).

49 Rebecca Bell-Metereau, *Hollywood Androgyny* (New York: Columbia University Press, 1985), p. 75.

50 Ibid., p. 73.

51 Gaines, 'The *Queen Christina* Tie-Ups', p. 43.

52 Alexander Walker, *The Celluloid Sacrifice: Aspects of Sex in the Movies* (New York: Hawthorn Books, 1967), p. 109.

53 Hopper, *From Under My Hat*, p. 200.

54 Samuel Marx, *Mayer and Thalberg* (New York: Random House, 1975), p. 148.

55 John Bainbridge, *Garbo* (New York: Doubleday & Company, 1955), p. 181.

56 Affron, *Cinema and Sentiment*, pp. 184–5.

57 Bell-Metereau, *Hollywood Androgyny*, p. 77.

58 Lewis Stone, Hedda Hopper file.

59 Terry Castle, *The Apparitional Lesbian: Female Homosexuality and Modern Culture* (New York: Columbia University Press, 1993).

60 Schatz, *The Genius of the System*, p. 254.

61 Rilla Page Palmborg, *The Private Life of Greta Garbo* (Garden City, NY: Doubleday, Doran & Company, 1931), p. 1.

62 Ibid., p. 5.

63 Andrew Britton, 'Stars and Genre', in Christine Gledhill (ed.), *Stardom: Industry of Desire* (London and New York: Routledge, 1991), p. 205.

64 Krutzen, *The Most Beautiful Woman*, p. 6.

65 Ibid., p. 125.

CREDITS

· ·

Queen Christina

USA
1933
Production company
Metro-Goldwyn-Mayer Ltd.
US release
28 December 1933
US Distributor
Loew's Distribution
UK release
3 September 1934
Distributor (UK)
Metro-Goldwyn-Mayer Ltd.
Copyright date
23 January 1934
New York premiere
26 December 1933
UK release
16 February 1934

Producer
Walter Wanger
Director
Rouben Mamoulian
Screenplay
Salka Viertel, H. M.
Harwood
Original Story
Salka Viertel, Margaret
LeVino
Dialogue
S. N. Behrman
**Photography
(black and white)**
William Daniels
Gaffer
Floyd Porter
Music Director
Herbert Stothart
Editor
Blanche Sewell
Art Director
Alexander Toluboff
Interior decoration
Edwin B. Willis
Costumes
Adrian
Recording director
Douglas Shearer
Mixer
Art Wilson
Still photographer
Clarence Bull
Sword fight staging
Fred Cavens
Historical adviser
Colonel Einhornung
103 Minutes
9,298 feet

Greta Garbo
Queen Christina
John Gilbert
Don Antonio
Lewis Stone
Axel Oxenstierna
Ian Keith
Magnus de la Gardie
Reginald Owen
*Prince Palatine Charles
Augustus*
Elizabeth Young
Ebba Sparre
C. Aubrey Smith
Aage
Gustav von Seyffertitz
General
David Torrence
Archbishop
Akim Tamiroff
Pedro
Cora Sue Collins
Little Christina
George Renavent
French Ambassador
Ferdinand Munier
Innkeeper
Edward Norris
Count Jacob de la Gardie
Barbara Barondess
Servant girl
Paul Hurst
Swedish soldier
Ed Gargan
Fellow drinker
Wade Boteler
Rabble-rouser

Credits checked by Markku
Salmi.
The print of *Queen Christina*
in the National Film and
Television Archive was
acquired specially for the
360 project from Turner
Entertainment.

ALSO PUBLISHED

If you would like further Information about future BFI Film Classics or about other books on film, media and popular culture from BFI Publishing, please write to:

BFI Film Classics
British Film Institute
21 Stephen Street
London
W1P 2LN

26

**BFI Publishing
21 Stephen Street
FREEPOST 7
LONDON
W1E 4AN**